1/09

26.00

DISCARD

The Forensic Entomologist

Other titles in the Crime Scene Investigations series:

The Forensic Entomologist

by Diane Yancey

LUCENT BOOKS
A part of Gale, Cengage Learning

GALE
CENGAGE Learning™

Detroit • New York • San Francisco • New Haven, Conn • Waterville, Maine • London

LIBRARY OF CONGRESS CATALOGING-IN-PUBLICATION DATA

Yancey, Diane.
   The forensic entomologist / by Diane Yancey.
     p. cm. — (Crime scene investigations)
   Includes bibliographical references and index.
   ISBN 978-1-4205-0070-7 (hardcover)
  1. Forensic entomology—Juvenile literature. I. Title.
   RA1063.45.Y36 2009
   614'.1—dc22

                               2008026587

Lucent Books
27500 Drake Rd
Farmington Hills MI 48331

ISBN-13: 978-1-4205-0070-7
ISBN-10: 1-4205-0070-8

Printed in the United States of America
1 2 3 4 5 6 7 12 11 10 09 08

Contents

Foreword

The popularity of crime scene and investigative crime shows on television has come as a surprise to many who work in the field. The main surprise is the concept that crime scene analysts are the true crime solvers, when in truth, it takes dozens of people, doing many different jobs, to solve a crime. Often, the crime scene analyst's contribution is a small one. One Minnesota forensic scientist says that the public "has gotten the wrong idea. Because I work in a lab similar to the ones on *CSI*, people seem to think I'm solving crimes left and right—just me and my microscope. They don't believe me when I tell them that it's just the investigators that are solving crimes, not me."

Crime scene analysts do have an important role to play, however. Science has rapidly added a whole new dimension to gathering and assessing evidence. Modern crime labs can match a hair of a murder suspect to one found on a murder victim, for example, or recover a latent fingerprint from a threatening letter, or use a powerful microscope to match tool marks made during the wiring of an explosive device to a tool in a suspect's possession.

Probably the most exciting of the forensic scientist's tools is DNA analysis. DNA can be found in just one drop of blood, a dribble of saliva on a toothbrush, or even the residue from a fingerprint. Some DNA analysis techniques enable scientists to tell with certainty, for example, whether a drop of blood on a suspect's shirt is that of a murder victim.

While these exciting techniques are now an essential part of many investigations, they cannot solve crimes alone. "DNA doesn't come with a name and address on it," says the Minnesota forensic scientist. "It's great if you have someone in custody to match the sample to, but otherwise, it doesn't help.

That's the investigator's job. We can have all the great DNA evidence in the world, and without a suspect, it will just sit on a shelf. We've all seen cases with very little forensic evidence get solved by the resourcefulness of a detective."

While forensic specialists get the most media attention today, the work of detectives still forms the core of most criminal investigations. Their job, in many ways, has changed little over the years. Most cases are still solved through the persistence and determination of a criminal detective whose work may be anything but glamorous. Many cases require routine, even mind-numbing tasks. After the July 2005 bombings in London, for example, police officers sat in front of video players watching thousands of hours of closed-circuit television tape from security cameras throughout the city, and as a result were able to get the first images of the bombers.

The Lucent Books Crime Scene Investigations series explores the variety of ways crimes are solved. Titles cover particular crimes such as murder, specific cases such as the killing of three civil rights workers in Mississippi, or the role specialists such as medical examiners play in solving crimes. Each title in the series demonstrates the ways a crime may be solved, from the various applications of forensic science and technology to the reasoning of investigators. Sidebars examine both the limits and possibilities of the new technologies and present crime statistics, career information, and step-by-step explanations of scientific and legal processes.

The Crime Scene Investigations series strives to be both informative and realistic about how members of law enforcement—criminal investigators, forensic scientists, and others—solve crimes, for it is essential that student researchers understand that crime solving is rarely quick or easy. Many factors—from a detective's dogged pursuit of one tenuous lead to a suspect's careless mistakes to sheer luck to complex calculations computed in the lab—are all part of crime solving today.

The Bug Detectives

Distinguished university professor Bernard Greenberg never dreamed he would help solve crimes when he began studying insects in graduate school in the late 1940s. In 1976, however, he was unexpectedly drawn into the world of violence and murder when police found the corpses of two men in an abandoned building in Chicago. The badly decomposed bodies had been wrapped in blankets and hidden in a closet. The investigation that followed revealed that the men had been killed by neighborhood drug dealers who blamed them for a police raid a few days before.

The suspects were arrested and held for trial. One even agreed to cooperate and provide details of the murders in exchange for a lighter sentence. But as the trial approached, the district attorney (DA) realized that he did not have scientific confirmation of time of death. The bodies had been too decayed for that to be determined by a medical examiner using traditional means such as body temperature, livor mortis (settling of blood to the lower portion of the body, causing a purplish-red discoloration of the skin), and rigor mortis (stiffening of the body after death). The testimony of the one cooperating suspect was not enough. The DA wanted to make sure the jury would convict.

Searching for a solution, the DA called Greenberg, an entomologist at the University of Chicago. Entomologists study insects, which includes flies, beetles, crickets, mosquitoes, butterflies, and bees as well as other arthropods such as centipedes, scorpions, ticks, and mites. Greenberg specialized in blowflies. The DA asked him if he could determine the postmortem interval (PMI), the time between death and the discovery of the bodies. The victims had long since been buried, but the professor agreed to look at photographs of the crime scene. The photographs showed that maggots were on the bodies. Greenberg easily recognized the maggots as immature green bottle flies, a type of blowfly that arrives and lays eggs on a body within hours of death. "It's their living and they're good at it. There [are] not a lot of corpses lying around—they're at a premium— so they zero right in,"[1] he stated. He could also see by the location of the maggots on the body that many had finished feeding. Hard brown pupa cases indicated that they were going into the resting stage that comes just before they hatch into adults.

From experience, Greenberg knew that it took green bottle flies about two weeks to reach the pupa stage under laboratory

Entomologist Bernard Greenberg in his office at the University of Illinois in 1983.

9

Early Detectives

Bernard Greenberg was the first modern forensic entomologist, but he was not the first person to use insects to help solves crimes. In 1235 a Chinese death investigator identified a murderer by calling the men of a village together, asking them to bring the sickle each used to cut grain in the field. A man had been slashed to death, and, when the investigator observed blowflies swarming around the curved blade of one villager's tool, he knew they were attracted by the victim's blood and flesh. "The sickles of the others in the crowd have no flies," he told the owner. "Now you have killed a man ... so the flies gather."

In the 1800s, forensic entomologist and veterinarian Jean Pierre Megnin helped medical examiners and pathologists determine time of death through his study of insects that came and went on corpses according to predictable timelines. In 1935 entomologist Alexander Mearns used maggot larvae to help solve the Buck Ruxton double-murder case in Scotland. In 1956 in Hungary, entomologist Ferenc Mihalyi used maggots found on a corpse to clear a ferryboat captain of a murder for which he was accused. It was Greenberg, however, who finally developed the science into a recognized field on which others would base their careers.

Jessica Snyder Sachs, *Corpse: Nature, Forensics, and the Struggle to Pinpoint Time of Death*. Cambridge, MA: Perseus, 2001, p. 70.

conditions. He also knew that fly activity was affected by a variety of factors, particularly heat and cold. So he carefully checked weather conditions for Chicago around the alleged time of death. Using recorded temperatures and the fact that the maggots had begun to form pupa, Greenberg made his determination. It matched the date given by the cooperating suspect. Testifying to his conclusions in court, he became the first entomologist to act as an expert witness at a murder trial. All three defendants were convicted, and Greenberg observed,

"I'm happy to apply what I know to something that's as important as this, something that can lead to a conviction or acquittal. It's very satisfying to see justice done."[2]

Pioneers in the Field

Greenberg went on to help police in dozens of other homicide cases. That and his further research relating entomology to crime eventually earned him the title "The Father of Forensic Entomology." Forensic entomology differs from entomology in that it is the study of insects as they relate to legal processes. Three subdivisions of forensic entomology exist: urban (pest infestations in buildings or gardens), stored products (claims that a fly was found in a can of soup or maggots in a deli sandwich), and medicocriminal (insects helping to solve murder, suicide, rape, physical abuse, and contraband trafficking cases). Crime scene investigation focuses on medicocriminal cases.

Greenberg was just the first of a small but dedicated group of scientists who have pioneered the field of forensic entomology since the 1970s. In the United States, E. Paul Catts earned a master's degree in entomology at the University of Delaware in 1957 and became the chair of entomology at Washington State University in Pullman, Washington, in 1980. There he wrote and lectured widely on the subject of forensic entomology, and worked on more than fifty homicide cases with police before his death in 1996.

One of Catts's students, Wayne Lord, graduated from the University of Delaware in 1979 and went on to become the FBI's chief forensic entomologist and head of the Child Abduction and Serial Murder Investigations Unit. Lord is one of the first people that police contact when they need entomological assistance.

In Greenberg's Footsteps

Madison Lee (M. Lee) Goff, a former soldier who completed his doctor of philosophy degree (PhD) in entomology at the University of Hawaii in 1977, was another who followed in

Dr. Neal Haskell, holding a blowfly, became the first entomologist in the United States to earn a master's of science degree in forensic entomology.

Greenberg's footsteps. Goff became a forensic entomologist in 1983; became head of the forensic science program at Chaminade University of Honolulu, Hawaii, in 2001; and has participated in over 250 criminal investigations worldwide. In 2000 he became an adviser to the hit television series *CSI: Crime Scene Investigation*. He says of the program: "I mainly answer questions about whether a scenario could work—or how the production team could make it work better. It's always along the lines of 'a body is found on a mountain, buried up to its neck. What would happen to the body in those conditions; what insects would be present?'"[3]

In 1989 Neal Haskell became the first entomologist in the United States to earn a master's of science degree in forensic entomology. In 1993 he became the first to earn a PhD in the

Hitchhiking Bugs

Along with murder, suicide, and abuse, medicocriminal entomology deals with drug smuggling. Entomologist Trevor Crosby became the key to solving a smuggling case when New Zealand police asked him to look for insects on samples of marijuana they had confiscated during a large drug bust in 1988. Chemists had already analyzed the plants and found no compound that identified them as foreign grown varieties, but police were convinced they had been illegally imported into the county.

Crosby and his colleague Charles Watt, both employees of a New Zealand environmental research firm, carefully examined the marijuana and found sixty-one dried beetles and wasps trapped in the plants' buds. Only one insect—a rice weevil—was commonly found in New Zealand. Eight species were native only to Asia. The two men studied and compared the geographic locales for each species, drew a map of the area where they all overlapped, and concluded that the marijuana had come from a region approximately 186 miles (299km) northwest of Bangkok, Thailand. The drug dealers were charged not only with possession of an illegal substance but also with smuggling, a much more serious charge. "We didn't realize until after the trial that the police had no case without us," Crosby said. "[Without our input,] the case would have fallen around their ears."

Quoted in Rick Weiss, "Bug-Busters; the Insect Detectives," *Washington Post*, August 14, 1988.

same field. He has assisted law enforcement teams throughout North America with some seven hundred cases and teaches at St. Joseph's College in Indiana. He remembers being drawn to the world of forensics from his first exposure to it. "One day a local detective called me who knew I'd majored in entomology in college and said, 'Hey, Neal, we got a body at the morgue with insects on it. You wanna give it a shot?' The corpse turned out to be a guy I used to have breakfast with, and there were maggots in his teeth. Then I found some in his eyes, and I thought, 'This is want I want to do. This is just way too cool.' ... I've done an awful lot of neat things in my life. But this maggot work and getting the bad guys off the street is the neatest."[4]

Outside the United States, Gail Anderson heads the Forensic Entomology Laboratory, established in 1999 at Simon Fraser University in British Columbia, Canada. In addition to helping police solve cases, she studies flesh-eating insects native to her country, many of which have never been studied before. German forensic entomologist Mark Benecke, nicknamed "Dr. Maggot" by his associates, works internationally on forensic cases as a freelance insect expert. He is also a visiting professor at police academies and universities in Germany, England, Vietnam, Colombia, and the Philippines. Noted British forensic entomologist Zakaria Erzinçlioğlu was a widely recognized expert on blowflies and helped police solve over two hundred murders in England before his death in 2002.

Pressing Forward

In an effort to promote the highest educational, ethical, and performance standards in the field, ten leading forensic entomologists founded the American Board of Forensic Entomology (ABFE) in 1996. Original members included Catts, Lord, Goff, Haskell, Valerie Cervenka, Robert Hall, K.C. Kim, Kenneth Schoenly, Theodore Suman, and Jeffrey Wells. The ABFE is the body that awards certification to a forensic entomologist, attesting to his or her high level of expertise in the area of medicocriminal entomology. In 2004 the North American Forensic

Before the growth of forensic entomology, maggots were just something pushed aside by investigators to get to the "real" evidence.

Entomology Association (NAFEA) was organized with the goal of providing opportunities for forensic entomologists to interact and collaborate. Both groups have drawn attention to the value of forensic entomology, as well as the need for more qualified workers in the field. As of 2008, there were fewer than seventy forensic entomologists worldwide, and less than half of those have a medicocriminal focus.

Even with their commitment to high standards, forensic entomologists have faced widespread skepticism. Their skills were not in great demand prior to the 1990s. "In the seventies or eighties, my superiors would have laughed at this [studying insect evidence]," says Pennsylvania state trooper Jim Shubzda, who attended a police entomology course led by K.C. Kim at Pennsylvania State University in 1999. "Maggots were just something we pushed aside to look at other stuff."[5]

The insect detectives were aware of such skepticism, and even sympathized with it. "It seems like science fiction, doesn't it?" comments Greenberg. "Who would ever think a fly could be a witness in a murder?"[6] Nevertheless, forensic entomologists were convinced that they had significant contributions to make, and they worked to educate the public about the value of maggots and other "creepy crawlies." They spoke to the FBI, at universities, and at forensic conferences. They offered seminars to police and crime scene investigators. Greenberg says, "Medical examiners and detectives are moving away from the traditional view that maggots are simply loathsome worms. They're coming to realize that insects can communicate and that they sometimes have much to say."[7]

A Valuable Tool

Understanding what insects are saying is easier said than done, however, and often stirs up controversy. Only a relatively few species have been studied in-depth, and many of the variables that affect their behavior are still a mystery, even to the entomologists themselves. Insect experts Amoret Brandt and Martin Hall note, "Forensic entomology is a relatively young science, so there are many areas which need further investigation."[8]

Despite skepticism and controversy, forensic entomology is earning a reputation as a valuable tool, simply because it helps solve crimes and bring criminals to justice. For the "bug detectives," that is enough for now. As Greenberg points out, "forensic entomology is not the silver bullet, but the more ways you have of looking at a case, the better."[9]

CHAPTER 1

Crime Scene Insects

Entomologist Bernard Greenberg of the University of Chicago was able to help police solve a double murder case in Chicago in 1976 because he was a blowfly expert. Hawaiian-based forensic entomologist M. Lee Goff was originally interested in acarology, the study of ticks and mites. Gail Anderson in British Columbia researches Canadian insects. Entomologists specialize because they cannot be familiar with every type of insect that exists. There are just too many. Insects are found on every continent worldwide, and more than 1 million species have been named and described. A possible 30 million more wait to be identified.

For practicality, forensic entomologists specialize in insects that are present at crime scenes. These range from the obvious flies to obscure soil-dwelling predators who feed on decomposition by-products. Goff states, "It is the job of the forensic entomologist to interpret the varied interactions between arthropods and the corpse, ... eliminating from consideration organisms that are present by accident."[10]

Even with that narrower focus, the range of species to be studied is vast. Depending on the geographic local, as many as six hundred species of insects can visit a corpse during the course of its decomposition. These include representatives from at least ten families of flies and eight families of beetles. Journalist Duane Bourne writes, "Within minutes [of death], insects flock to the body and flies lay eggs, which eventually turn into maggots. Then come successive invasions of ants, mites, spiders, and other critters. ... As many as 600 bugs will hover around a body [depending on conditions]."[11]

Succession

Scavengers such as coyotes, raccoons, and vultures are the most noticeable living things to prey on a corpse. Despite their size, however, they are not as numerous, as hungry, or as efficient as insects. Insects make up about 85 percent of all animal species that are found in any particular vicinity. In warm weather they can consume 60 percent of a corpse in less than a week. Forensic expert Emily Craig says, "There's a saying among forensic entomologists: Three flies and their offspring can consume a carcass as quickly as can a full-grown lion. Not bad for tiny creatures less than an inch long."[12]

Forensic entomologists know that of the insects that are attracted to a corpse, all arrive in a predictable order known as faunal (animal) succession. This means that, starting with flies, one group arrives first, settles in, and helps prepare the way for the next group to follow. "Some [insects] like you when you're

Blowfly maggots feed on calf liver during a study to determine the growth rates of the maggots at various temperatures.

fresh dead, some like you when you're in the bloat phase, and some like you when you're chewy,"[13] explains Australian forensic entomologist Ian Dadour.

The corpse is the primary attraction, but its presence creates a unique ecosystem that supports a variety of consumers. Those that eat the decaying flesh are known as necrophagous species and include flies and some types of beetles. Predators—usually beetles—feed on flies, their eggs, and their larvae. A mixed group feeds on both the corpse and on other predatory species. Finally, herbivores, attracted to decaying vegetation and fungi, live under and around the vicinity of a corpse. No matter what their involvement, each group changes the corpse and its environment in some way.

Blowflies, Soldier Flies, and Cheese Skippers

Of the necrophagous species, blowflies (family Calliphoridae) are usually in the first wave of insects to arrive on a corpse, often within ten minutes of death. Blowflies are closely followed by a variety of houseflies (family Muscidae) and flesh flies (family Sarcophagidae). All are drawn by the smell of volatile compounds that are released from the body in the earliest stages of decay. "You think a bloodhound has a keen sense of smell, but blowflies are superior in every way," says forensic entomologist Joe Keiper. "They have receptors that are homed in to find the first gases of decomposition."[14]

Blowflies, houseflies, and flesh flies prefer to infest moist tissue, so they land and examine the surface of the corpse while it is still warm. If the flesh is too dry, they go in search of something better. Forensic entomologist David Faulkner states, "Suitability for a fly usually requires that there's moisture available, [and] that there's an area that's hidden that may be dark, say the under surface of an area where it's not exposed to bright sunlight."[15]

A blowfly lays eggs on a dead rat. At a death scene, blowflies are usually the first insects to arrive at a corpse.

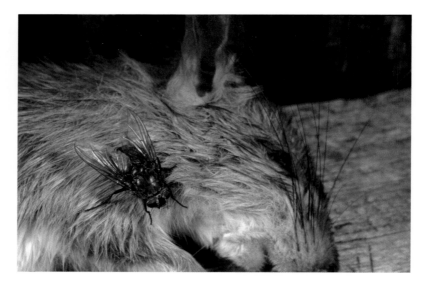

Soldier flies (*Hermetica illucens*) are necrophagous, as are cheese skippers (*Piophila casei*). Cheese skippers are also known as ham skippers or cheese flies because they infested improperly stored cheese and ham in earlier times, and because older larvae have been seen to "skip." When disturbed, they grab the folds of their own abdomens with their mouth hooks, tense their muscles, and then release their hold, flipping themselves up to 6 inches (15cm) in the air. Both species are attracted to the strong cheesy odors that a corpse gives off several days after death, so they are usually part of the second wave of arrivals. Haskell says, "They like it when it's goopy and yucky and in a putrefaction state or beyond, in a liquefaction stage."[16]

Cheese skippers played a role in solving the murder of a fifteen-year-old schoolgirl in England. The girl had last been seen alive in mid-May, and her body was found in an overgrown area behind her parent's house in late July. Police asked forensic entomologist Zakaria Erzinçlioğlu to give an estimate of time of death. The presence of fly pupa allowed him to say that death had occurred at least three weeks before. He also found cheese skipper larvae and larder beetles (*Dermestes lardaroius*), so named for their attraction to food stored in larders or pantries. Erzinçlioğlu knew that cheese skippers arrived at a body about two months

The Organization of Living Things

Taxonomy is the science dealing with the description, identification, naming, and classification of organisms. At least seven major ranks, or categories, are commonly used. In descending order, individuals in each category become more alike. For instan ce, kingdom Animalia contains both human beings and insects, but phylum Chordata is specific for humans and phylum Arthropoda is specific for insects.

An example of the taxonomy of the common housefly is as follows:

Kingdom:	Animalia
Phylum:	Arthropoda
Class:	Insecta
Order:	Diptera
Family:	Muscidae
Genus:	*Musca*
Species:	*domestica*

after death in the locale where the body was found. He said, "Both cheese skippers and the larder beetle larvae … [arrive] at a particular stage of protein putrefaction. Their presence, therefore, placed the minimum time of death at about the middle of May."[17] Police were later able to corroborate Erzinçlioğlu's conclusion when the fifteen-year-old killer, a friend of the victim, confessed to the crime.

A Variety of Beetles

When a corpse becomes too dry for flies, a variety of beetles arrives and takes their place. Some, such as rove beetles (family Staphylinidae), hister beetles (family Histeridae), and carrion beetles (family Silphidae) are predators, invading the corpse to feast on the eggs and maggots left behind by the flies. Others are necrophageous. These include the ham beetles (family

Cleridae) and skin/hide beetles (family Dermistidae) that feed on the drying skin, exposed tendons, and bones of the corpse. Hide beetles are the only beetles to secrete enzymes necessary for breaking down keratin, a protein component of hair. "They are sort of a cleanup operation,"[18] explains Greenberg.

Beetle evidence alone is seldom enough to bring a killer to justice, primarily because their life cycles are not as predictable as those of flies. In conjunction with other insect activity, however, beetles can be useful indicators. In 1996 in Hawaii, Goff's knowledge of beetles helped solve the case of a U.S. Marine found dead in a rain forest on the island of Oahu. The body was so decomposed that most of the flies had disappeared by the time Goff arrived on the scene, but he found numbers of beetles still on the corpse. He stated, "We had clerid beetles and hide beetles, both of which like their bodies slightly dried. I also found larvae of a rove beetle—it arrives early, but you don't see its larvae until a couple weeks into decomposition."[19]

Together with the presence of cheese skipper and soldier fly larvae, Goff was able to determine that the body had been in the forest between twenty-nine and thirty-one days. Military police detained and interrogated two Marines who had been with the victim during that time frame, and they confessed to the crime.

Small, but Numerous

While flies and beetles play major roles in crime scene investigation, wasps are minor players. Nevertheless, they can sometimes be found in great numbers and be very aggressive around a corpse. Part of the necrophagous/predator group, they eat adult flies, feed on fluids that come out of the body during decomposition, and also act as parasitoids of fly maggots. Parasitoids are insects that spend a significant portion of their life within a single host, but on reaching maturity become free-living entities. Tiny wasps of the families Pteromalidae, Chalcidae, and Diapriidae like to lay their eggs on fly maggots, so that when their larvae hatch, they kill and feed on the maggot's flesh before resting and developing into adults within its shell.

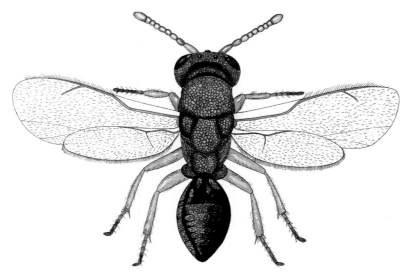

Parasitic wasps, such as this one, lay their eggs on fly maggots, and when their larvae hatch, they kill and feed on the maggot's flesh before developing into adults.

Like wasps, ants can be aggressive when they arrive at a body in large numbers. In one case, crime scene investigators came upon a corpse that appeared to have been outlined in white chalk. As they got closer, they discovered that the white lines were ants, carrying eggs and maggots away from the body and back to their nest.

At times, wasps' or ants' predatory activity can have a significant effect on the decomposition process. Adults of both groups have been known to carry away so many flies, eggs, and maggots that decomposition of the body is significantly slowed. Goff writes, "Whenever I see any species of social insects associated with a corpse, I have to consider whether their depredations [predatory attacks] have altered the normal pattern of decomposition."[20]

In certain instances, ants and wasps have been useful in helping to determine time of death long after flies and beetles have come and gone. In a January 1990 case, for example, the remains of a nest of paper wasps in a skull helped forensic entomologists determine that the victim had been dead at least eighteen months. Their chain of reasoning was based on the fact that maggots, not active in cold winter months, had fed on and cleaned out the skull in the summer of 1988, making way for the wasps that build their nests in the spring to inhabit

Bugs in the Water

Corpses in water attract aquatic insects, but forensic entomologists currently know little about this subdivision of their field. As journalist Rick Weiss explains in his article "Bug-Busters, the Insect Detectives," published in the Washington Post,

Some insects, such as mosquitoes, midges and caddis flies, have aquatic larval stages and don't walk on land or take to the air until they become adults. One such larva—a bright red, multisegmented midge in the family Chironomidae—lives mostly on the bottom of freshwater lakes and rivers and is frequently found on corpses that have been submerged for long periods of time. According to [forensic entomologist] Neal Haskell . . . chironomids may provide important information about the PMI since they rarely appear on a floating body unless the corpse has already spent some time on the bottom.

Haskell emphasizes that little is known about the timing and development of aquatic, meat-eating insects, and much more research is needed. Still, medical investigators are beginning to take note of aquatic larvae on corpses, and are less frequently making the mistake one pathologist made in a [1989] Indiana murder case where a chironomid larva was misidentified as a red carpet fiber.

Rick Weiss, "Bug-Busters; the Insect Detectives," *Washington Post*, August 14, 1988.

it in 1989. The wasps had moved out as cold weather again approached in late 1989, leaving the nest empty as it had been found in early 1990.

In a 1994 case, analysis of an ant colony in a skull allowed a forensic entomologist to say that the colony had been in existence about twelve months. Taken in conjunction with fly and beetle pupae around the rest of the remains, the entomologist was able to give a tentative time of death, and police eventually tracked down the killer.

Soil Dwellers

Unlike ants that prey on fly eggs and maggots, soil-dwelling insects are drawn by compounds that leach into the earth as the body breaks down. Goff explains: "Fluid by-products [of decomposition] seep into the soil under the body. ... These fluids provide nutrients for a large number of ... decomposition-associated organisms present in the soil."[21] Many of these organisms are so small they can only be seen under a microscope.

Mites are some of the most common insects to be found in the ground under a corpse. Macrocheles mites are common in the early stages of decomposition, feeding on algae and fungi that grow in the dark, sodden environment. Later, Tyroglyphidae and Oribatidae mites arrive to feed on dry skin that falls to the ground as the body further decays.

Other organisms such as scorpions and symphylids (resembling centipedes) can be found in the soil under the body. Tiny soil beetles and springtails (six-legged, wingless arthropods) are also drawn to the seepage. The habits of these insects have not been studied adequately to determine exactly when they arrive and when they disperse, but finding them in the soil can indicate that a corpse was present long after the body has decayed away. Goff says, "There is no definite end to this stage ... and there may be carrion-associated species present in the soil fauna for several months or even years after death, depending on local conditions."[22]

Basic Entomology

In addition to being able to identify insects and larvae found on and around a corpse, forensic entomologists must be familiar with each species' life stages and be able to determine the stage of development larvae have reached when they are collected. This is basic entomology, so most have no difficulty in doing so.

Mites are some of the most common insects to be found in the ground under a corpse. The Oribatidae ground mite, for example, feeds on dry skin that falls off a decaying body.

Biologist Lawrence Kobilinsky says, "I only know a few forensic entomologists, but those that I know are true professionals. They are generally university types, they have been studying entomology for years, they understand the succession in the life cycle of these insects."[23]

Most forensically important insects are homometabolous, that is, they undergo complete metamorphosis during their life cycles. This means that adults lay eggs that hatch into larvae known as caterpillars, grubs, or maggots. The larvae look nothing like the adult insect. In contrast, hemimetabolous insects such as aphids, grasshoppers, and cockroaches do not undergo complete metamorphosis. Their eggs hatch into nymphs, which look like immature adults. These nymphs shed their skins as they mature and grow larger, but they always appear similar to adults.

In the homometabolous group, all larvae have an outer covering known as an exoskeleton. This exoskeleton is made of chitin, a protein material similar to fingernails. Larvae start out small, and in the course of their growth, all shed their exoskeleton, a process known as molting. Forensic expert Bill

Coffin Flies

The coffin fly, a species of scuttle fly, is a tiny, hunchbacked insect whose presence on a corpse tells entomologists that the body was once buried. In his book, Maggots, Murder, and Men, *the late forensic entomologist Zakaria Erzinçlioğlu describes the coffin fly's surprising ability to live underground:*

A number of scuttle fly species have the uncanny ability to find buried corpses, though how they do this is not fully understood. There is also a great deal of evidence to show that they can pass their entire life cycle underground, and, indeed, go through a number of generations deep in the soil. ...

Dr. Henry Disney, an authority on scuttle flies, conducted an interesting experiment by burying the carcasses of white mice in his vegetable garden in Cambridge, [England]. I was with him when he dug up the carcasses some weeks later. Although the topsoil was loose and crumbly, as one would expect in a vegetable garden, the lower levels in which the mice were buried were composed of a heavy clay. When we cracked open the clods of clay to extract the remains of the carcasses, large numbers of scuttle flies swarmed out. It is difficult to see how these minute flies could have gone about their business in the heavy, sticky clay without getting their legs and wings clogged up, but clearly they were able to come and go freely, presumably through pores and cracks in the clay.

Zakaria Erzinçlioğlu, *Maggots, Murder, and Men: Memories and Reflections of a Forensic Entomologist.* New York: Thomas Dunne, 2002, p. 181.

Bass and science writer Jon Jefferson explain: "When maggots first hatch, they're smaller than grains of rice; by the time they mature, they're roughly as long and fat as pieces of macaroni."[24] The developmental stages between molts are known as instars. Most fly larvae go through three instars, while beetle instars are more variable in number.

Soft and Sausage-Shaped

The larval forms of homometabolous insects vary in size, color, and anatomy. When it comes to beetle larvae, they look so different that they are relatively easy to identify. For instance, rove beetle larvae look somewhat like centipedes, with a hard, shiny-brown segmented body and a large head. Carrion beetle larvae are larger and dark brown with small legs. Scarab beetle larvae (family Scarabaeidae), usually found in the latest stages of decay, are fat and cream-colored.

Fly larvae, known as maggots, are more difficult to identify by species. All are small and legless. All have soft, sausage-shaped bodies that are cream colored and hairless. All move by contracting and extending their bodies, eat using mouth hooks which rake in decaying flesh, and breathe through two pairs of openings called spiracles. Spiracles are located near the head and on the posterior ends of their bodies, and, in some cases, the posterior set is distinctive enough to allow for identification. Author Jessica Snyder Sachs explains, "The ... spiracles of a blow fly maggot resemble ... a pair of scalloped sand dollars, each embossed with a cluster of lacy, petallike slits fanned around an inner 'button.' By comparison the spiracles of a flesh fly maggot appear somewhat less symmetrical, with broken rims surrounding a coarse set of slitted cracks."[25]

In order to be sure of the species they have in hand, however, forensic entomologists always collect maggots from a corpse and rear them to adults which have more distinctive features.

In order to determine the stage of development that fly maggots have reached, entomologists check their size and the number of spiracles they have. Newly hatched first-instar maggots are roughly 0.08 inches (0.2cm) long, and they grow to 0.2 inches (0.5cm) before molting the first time. They have a single slit in each spiracle. Second-instar maggots have two slits in each spiracle, and grow to around 0.4 inches (1cm) before they molt to become third-instar larvae. Third-instar maggots have three slits in their spiracles, and grow to between 0.6 and 0.8 inches (1.5cm–2cm) before entering the pupa stage.

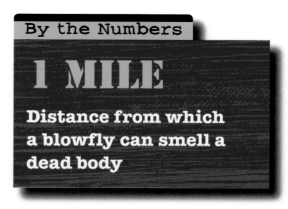

By the Numbers

1 MILE

Distance from which a blowfly can smell a dead body

Resting Stage

After going through their instars, larvae enter the pre-pupa stage where they stop eating and begin moving away from the corpse in order to prepare for the resting stage known as pupation. Within the protection of the case known as a pupa or cocoon, they transform into adults. Pre-pupa larvae may move hundreds of feet away from the body, forming trails as they migrate. Keiper says, "If you're a maggot, you don't want to form your pupa … right on the carcass. Coyote, raccoon, skunk, and other large scavengers some along and start feeding on the carrion, and if you're just sitting there, you're fair game. … This is a huge mystery—how they know where to go. They're not thinking animals. There are certain cues in the environment, could be sunlight or temperature, humidity, shade, pheromones [chemical signals]. We don't really know."[26]

The pupal stage begins as the larvae become shorter and thicker. At the same time, their skin becomes hard and forms a tough, protective case. With flies, the pupae are tiny and football shaped; resistant to heat, cold, wet, and dry environments; and unattractive to predators. Goff notes, "At first, the color of the pupa is similar to the white to yellow color of the maggot, but over the next few hours, the cuticle darkens to a deep reddish brown. You can get some idea of the age of the pupa during this period from the color of the pupal case."[27] During

To protect themselves from scavengers, pre-pupa larvae move away from a decaying body as they prepare for the pupal stage.

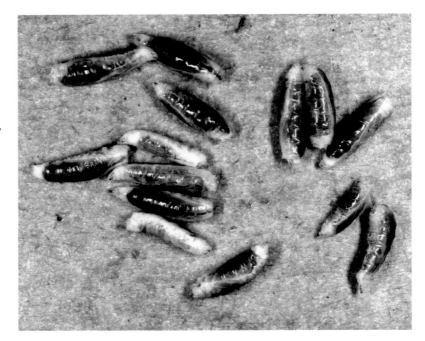

pupation, which can last up to six months, maggots morph into adult flies. When they are ready to emerge from the pupa, they pop open the top and pull themselves out, looking somewhat like pale spiders that skitter around the floor. Goff states, "To be able to get out of the pupal case, the fly must be soft and pliable; its cuticle is light in color and soft, and its wings are wrinkled and collapsed. Over a period of several hours, the cuticle hardens, the fly assumes its adult coloration, the wings expand, and the fly becomes fully functional."[28]

The study of flies seems like unpleasant work to some, but it is nothing compared to encounters with corpses, maggots, and the stink of decay that forensic entomologists regularly endure. FBI entomologist Wayne Lord admits, "We deal with things on a daily basis that no person should ever have to see. There are sights and sounds and smells that are unthinkable."[29] The work is not for everyone, and the bug experts are the first to acknowledge that. Nevertheless, they would not want to do anything else. Goff says, "We get to do things that people quite often run away from. Being a little weird is a good thing."[30]

CHAPTER 2

A Gruesome Business

Although they regularly face some of the most shocking and horrifying scenes imaginable, forensic entomologists find their profession fascinating, challenging, and rewarding. "Insects for me have been a magic carpet,"[31] says forensic entomologist Bernard Greenberg, referring to years of crime solving and travel to exotic places related to his profession.

Inevitably, there are aspects of the work that anger them and make them want to lash out at the perpetrators. Forensic entomologist James Olson says, "You see the sordid side. You think, 'How could one human being treat another this way?'"[32] As part of a criminal investigating team, however, they have to put whatever feelings they have on hold. They must think clearly and remain objective even when faced with flies swarming over a young woman's face or maggots feasting on the remains of a child. Forensic entomologist M. Lee Goff states, "I usually manage to cope by dissociating myself from the fact that I am working on what was once another human being. I attempt to … view the corpse as a specimen to be examined rather than as a person who has, in most cases, spent the last minutes or hours of life in pain and terror."[33]

Death and Decay

To a layperson, a blackened and bloated body is the stuff of nausea and nightmares. What was once a human being now resembles something out of a horror movie, rank and decomposing. "It's gruesome," forensic entomologist Joe Keiper concedes. "Nobody wants to end up like this."[34]

Unlike laypersons, however, forensic entomologists see decomposition as a process to be studied and better understood.

They even divide it into stages, which they use as reference points. Goff explains, "The value [of these stages] becomes particularly apparent when one is faced with the task of explaining to a jury a series of events associated with a murder and the subsequent decomposition of a body."[35]

Different experts categorize decomposition differently. Some divide the process into three stages——early, advancing, and advanced. Some prefer four—fresh, bloat, decay, and dry. Many, however, break it down into five because that allows for the greatest precision. The five stages are fresh, bloated, decay, postdecay, and skeletal.

Breakdown

The fresh stage of decomposition occurs during the first three days following death. Bacteria that are always present in the body's digestive system begin to digest the intestines, then break out and start digesting the surrounding organs. At the same time, flies lay their eggs around wounds and natural body openings including the mouth, nose, eyes, anus, and genitalia. These eggs, which number in the thousands and look like piles of sawdust, soon hatch into maggots which begin to eat their way into the body, further breaking it down. Forensic entomologist Richard Merritt says, "When the larvae start developing and feeding on the corpse, … they're just a feeding machine."[36]

Between days four and ten, the body goes through the bloated stage. Inside, bacteria break down tissues and cells and produce various foul-smelling gases, including hydrogen sulphide, methane, cadaverine, and putrescine. These gases build and create pressure which inflates the body, causing it to swell. The skin becomes stretched and shiny and assumes a green-black hue. At the same time, tens of thousands of growing maggots continue eating their way into the head, chest, and abdomen. They often move as a mass, benefiting from communal heat and shared digestive secretions. Forensic expert Bill Bass and science writer Jon Jefferson observe, "As maggots digest human tissue, the chemical breakdown of the flesh

Becoming a Forensic Entomologist

Job Description:
A forensic entomologist studies insects found at crime scenes in order to help answer questions about the postmortem interval (PMI), whether the body had been moved, and how the victim died. Work takes place both in the laboratory and in the field. In addition to aiding law enforcement officials, forensic entomologists often teach and perform research at a college or university, act as consultants, and provide continuing education classes to law enforcement officials. Forensic entomologists are often asked to testify in court as expert witnesses.

Education:
Aspiring forensic entomologists must earn a bachelor of science degree in biology, zoology, or entomology, plus a master's degree in entomology from an accredited college or university. Most forensic entomologists also earn a PhD in entomology and become certified by the American Board of Forensic Entomology.

Qualifications:
Aspiring forensic entomologists must be objective, persistent, and enjoy solving puzzles. They must be able to handle situations involving death and decay that others avoid. They must have a sense of humor.

Salary:
$40,000 to $85,000 per year

generates a surprising amount of heat; on cold mornings … it's not uncommon to see steam rising off a writhing mass of maggots huddled together for warmth."[37]

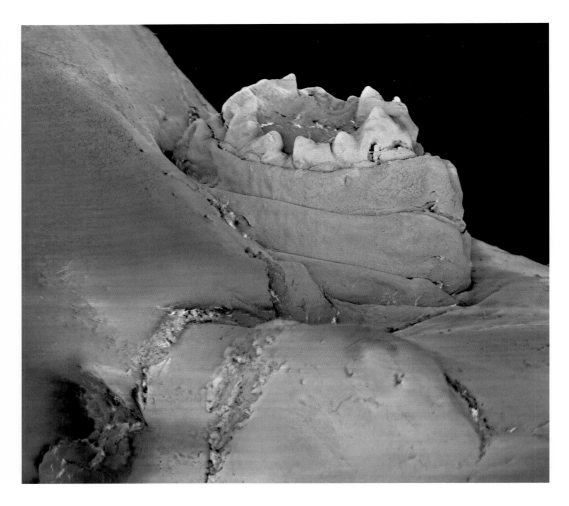

An electron micrograph of a blowfly maggot (larva) feeding on liver tissue.

Other insects contribute to the body's breakdown at this stage, too. "As decomposition continues, we find a more varied assemblage of arthropods becoming involved in the decomposition process,"[38] says Goff. These include the flesh flies and carrion beetles which are attracted by the gas and body fluids.

"The Stink Is the Worst"

The decay stage occurs sometime between days ten and twenty, depending on environmental conditions. As skin and tissues break down due to bacterial decay, the bloated body collapses into a flattened mass of slimy flesh. The exposed parts such as hands and feet become black, and there is a very strong smell of decay. "The stink is the worst," says forensic entomologist Neal Haskell. "You never get used to the smell of decomposition. It's meant to make you gag and throw up."[39] Fly maggots continue to consume the moist flesh during this stage. They are joined by more larvae of predatory beetles.

During the postdecay stage (days twenty to fifty) cheese flies consume any moist flesh that might remain. The body dries, becoming a tangled mass of bones, cartilage, and skin. Skin beetles, hide beetles, and wasps feed on the drying remains. Keiper says, "They love ... dry, leathery skin, and they'll break that down for a couple of months."[40] A rancid smell, caused when the decaying organic material releases butyric acid, persists.

By the final skeletal stage (days 50 to 365), the body is dry and consists of little more than bones and hair. Moths, mites, and bacteria feed on it and each other until only bones remain. "In the end, nothing rests next to the white bones but a sort of brown earth, finely granular, composed of insect pupal cases ... and the excrement of successive generations of insects,"[41] describes French entomologist Jean Pierre Megnin.

At the Scene

Despite the repulsive sights and smells, forensic entomologists take every opportunity to go to a crime scene to collect insects. There they can see firsthand the environmental conditions, how the body is positioned, where the insects are on the body, and that no evidence is overlooked. With so few forensic entomologists in the world, however, most live too far away to visit a scene in person. Thus, most rely on CSI teams to collect material for them and send it to their labs.

Members of CSI teams are encouraged to attend classes on insect collection so that they know exactly how the process should be carried out. Goff explains, "The way evidence is collected can present a number of problems the forensic entomologist must cope with. I frequently receive shipments of insects that

Processing a Crime Scene

The proper method to process a crime scene for insect evidence is as follows:

1 Secure the scene to prevent contamination.

2 Document the scene with sketches, notes, and photos.

3 Stand and observe insect evidence around the body, noting types of insects and locations.

4 Collect flying insects by making five to six sweeps of the area around and above the body using a large insect net. These insects should be killed on-site and preserved for later identification.

5 Collect samples of eggs and live larvae at various stages. Preserve samples of each for later examination. Store at least one of each type for transport.

6 Take and record temperatures in and around the body, including air temperature, temperature at the surface, and internal body temperature.

7 Take and record temperature of maggot masses.

8 After body is removed, take and record soil temperature.

9 Collect soil samples under and up to 3 feet (0.9 meter) away from where the body was.

10 Obtain meteorological data for the area, including peak high and low temperatures at the location where the body was.

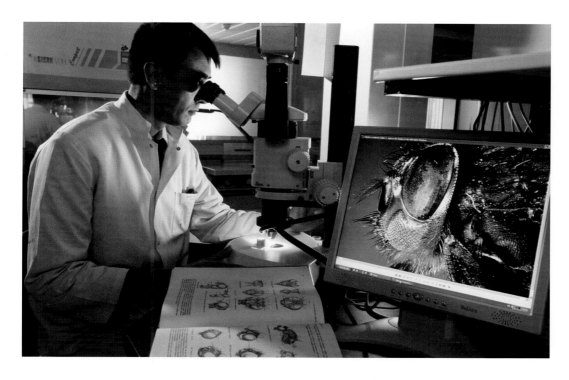

have been collected from corpses by people who fail to document where on the body, and sometimes even when, they gathered them. ... Then there is a real danger of misinterpretation."[42]

Crime scene technicians learn that they must photograph everything possible at the scene, ranging from trees and bushes near the corpse to insects on the body. Once documentation is finished, they must collect adult specimens, taking care not to scare away any that are flying or crawling around the corpse. They must also learn which larvae to collect, focusing first on the oldest stage of each possible species. Journalist Claudia Dreifus explains, "The mantra [formula] is, you collect the largest larvae, because they'll be the oldest. If you have 4-day-old insects, the body has usually been dead four days."[43] Smaller, less-developed larvae cannot be automatically rejected, however, because the presence of different instars can mean that more than one wave of flies has visited the body, or that the first generation of flies has developed and laid their eggs again on the body, and the second generation is underway.

Most forensic entomologists would welcome the chance to go to a crime scene and collect evidence. With so few forensic entomologists in the world, however, most of their work is conducted in a lab while crime scene investigators collect their case samples.

Collecting Difficulties

Sometimes collecting insects is difficult due to the location of the corpse. It can be lying on a precarious slope where investigators have to clamber over rocks to reach it, or in the midst of heavy brush that must be carefully cut back so as not to destroy evidence. It can be hidden in an airless closet or stuffed in the

Capturing flying specimens around a corpse in butterfly nets—without disturbing evidence at the surrounding crime scene—can be challenging.

crawl space under a house. FBI entomologist Wayne Lord says, "Try crawling up under a porch in 85 or 90 degree heat to inspect a body that's been lying there for a few days. After a while, you just learn to suck it up."[44]

Collecting can also be extremely time-consuming because of the many specimens involved. Around one corpse, Goff identified the remains of at least twenty-five different kinds of insects that included blowflies; hister, rove, and scarab beetles; moth flies; tailless whip scorpions; and mites. He remarked, "Not one of these had been actively involved throughout the entire decomposition process, but each of them had played a significant role in decomposition at a specific time."[45]

Capturing flying specimens—flies, wasps, and moths— is challenging, too, especially when using a butterfly net. Investigators must practice to become successful at skimming the net over the corpse, then twisting it to trap the insects inside. An alternate approach involves setting out adhesive material like flypaper on which insects become stuck. Once trapped, specimens must be placed in a killing jar, a screw-top container with plaster of paris saturated with a killing agent such as ethyl acetate on the bottom. They are later carefully removed, mounted for viewing, and packaged for shipping if necessary.

Samples of Everything

After adult specimens are collected, attention shifts to specimens in other stages of life that are on the body and the ground. Samples are first taken from the maggot masses, a task that can be hard for the inexperienced to face. Forensic expert Emily Craig explains why: "Thousands of maggots can accumulate in a dead victim's chest cavity or pelvis, sort of like a chicken carcass packed tight with lots of creamy overcooked

> **By the Numbers**
>
> # 48,000
>
> **Number of maggots found on a 5.5 ounce piece of meat after 24 hours**

The Right Equipment

When forensic entomologists visit a crime scene, they must be prepared to collect and store insect evidence. That involves bringing the following articles:

gloves
camera
thermometers
aquatic net bag
insect net
forceps or tweezers
spoons
trowels
Ziploc bags, vials, and other collection containers
80 percent ethanol solution
sand and chunks of raw liver
killing jars and killing agent
field spotlights

rice. Then the maggots pull together into a cohesive group that churns and boils continually."[46] When they are so numerous, the squirming larvae are scooped up with a spoon. If not, they can be gently brushed off the body into a container or picked up with special tweezers.

Beetle larvae, shed skins, and pupa cases are collected using tweezers, too. About half of the living larvae and maggots are killed by being plunged in hot water and then transferred to a solution of 80 percent ethanol which prevents discoloration and shrinkage. These represent the specimens' stage of development at collection. Goff notes, "The clock is started with the invasion of the insects and is stopped by the collection and preservation of insects from the corpse. Each stage of development … represents a distinct interval of time on that clock—hours, days, months, or possibly years."[47] The rest of the living larvae are placed in paper containers with food—usually raw liver—and air holes so they will survive until they reach the lab.

After insects are collected, the body—or what is left of it—is carefully placed in a zippered body bag and removed. Investigators then collect evidence that had been under the body. This involves picking up insects, larvae, and pupae that can be clearly seen as well as those that are hiding in leaves, bark, and humus. A trowel is used to scoop up samples of soil, too. The soil is later processed to isolate specimens too small to be picked up with tweezers.

In the Morgue

Collection does not end at the crime scene. The body is transported to the morgue, where an autopsy takes place. An autopsy is an examination to determine cause of death. If the autopsy cannot be performed right away, the body is stored in a cold chamber in the morgue, where temperatures are kept low enough to stop the development of any maggots that are present. Otherwise they will continue to devour the corpse until there is little left for the medical examiner to look at.

During the autopsy, the medical examiner, or attending forensic entomologist, continues collecting every insect and larval species. Body openings are examined in particular because they are favorite sites of infestation. Like in the field, half the living maggots are killed and preserved, while half are placed in containers with air and food. Notes are taken regarding where the specimens were located on the corpse and their stages of development.

Packaging and Shipping

If a forensic entomologist is not present at the crime scene, the recovered insects must be packaged and shipped to him or her for analysis. Crime scene technicians and medical examiners

In "maggot motels" like this one, breeding is helped by a constant air flow and an available food source, like pieces of raw liver.

are taught that insect specimens are delicate and must be transported according to established procedures. "Our forensic folks are trained to package the bugs. There is a certain way that it has to be done,"[48] says Hiram Bustamante, spokesperson for the Orange County Sheriff's Office in Orlando, Florida .

In the past, specimens were not always shipped correctly. Insect experts would receive boxes or bags of dead, dried flies and larvae, from which they were asked to determine species and age. Depending on the condition of the specimens, the help insect experts could give was limited. Forensic entomologist Haskell remembers, "We used to get bugs sent to us for identification. … All in nice little letter envelopes with return addresses. First the people [who collected the bugs] would swat them, then they would take them to the post office, where they'd get cancelled. I'd open them up and there would be these little squished legs and wings. You don't want to do that."[49]

Today, crime scene technicians carefully pack all specimens in proper containers for shipping, making sure that the living larvae have enough food and air to make the trip alive. They box up soil taken from the crime scene and organize paperwork that includes photos, autopsy results, collection times and locations, and temperatures at collection and during transit. Packages are sent by Express Mail or overnight delivery so that they are received as quickly as possible. Without such precautions, there is the risk that the specimens will die during transport.

Maggot Motels and Berlese Funnels

Once they receive the samples, forensic entomologists follow their own established procedures to identify and analyze the specimens. Living larvae require quick attention. They are placed in rearing chambers, nicknamed "maggot motels," with air and food, again usually pieces of raw liver. The chambers are programmed to maintain temperatures that support development, commonly around 79°F (26°C). They can also be programmed to mimic periods of daylight and darkness, with twelve hours of light and twelve hours of darkness being a common schedule. While the immature specimens grow to adulthood, they are closely watched and their development is recorded. Once adults hatch, their species can then be determined and used for further analysis.

In addition to raising maggots, forensic entomologists must separate and identify any tiny insects that are living in soil samples taken from the crime scene. To do this they use a Berlese funnel, named after Italian scientist Antonio Berlese, who designed the device in the 1800s to aid in his study of mites and ticks. Relatively simple, the funnel is a large cone-shaped utensil with fine wire mesh screen stretched across its mouth. It works on the principle that soil-dwelling insects prefer cool, dark conditions and will move away from warmth and light.

To use the funnel, forensic entomologists place samples of soil and leaf litter from around the corpse on the screen. The funnel is placed under a heat/light source, usually a simple light bulb. The warmth and brightness above causes insects to migrate downward, where they fall through the screen and out of the funnel tube into a container of ethanol placed below. Goff explains, "Leave this in place about twenty-four to forty-eight hours, and you will [have] … effectively extracted virtually all the soil-dwelling insects that are present in the sample."[50]

Studying pupal cases, such as the empty pupal case pictured here, is important because the cases indicate a stage of development that might otherwise be missed.

"Pupal Cases Nailed Him"

When examining soil samples, forensic entomologists are always alert for pupal cases, which look like pellets and can be easily mistaken for small animal droppings. The dry, hardened containers are important because they indicate a stage of

development that might otherwise be missed. If the cases are round at both ends, the adult insect has not emerged, and its species can sometimes be identified. Goff explains, "Forensic entomologists have … begun to devise various methods for determining the age of pupae, including dissections to determine the age of the developing fly inside."[51] If the ends appear to have been cut off and the interiors are hollow, a complete life cycle has taken place, and the pupae may be the only evidence that a species has come and gone from the corpse. Goff also points out, "If any [empty pupal cases] are present, at least one generation of flies has completed development and left the corpse."[52]

In the year 2000, the discovery of pupal cases resulted in the difference between freedom and prison for a Louisiana killer. On November 5, 1993, three members of the Perry family—Darryl, Annie, and four-year-old Krystal—were found dead in a cabin where they had been vacationing in Mississippi. Forensic expert Bass was shown photos of insect activity on the victims, and until he spotted tiny brown pupae casings in Krystal's hair, he believed that the fly maggots he saw were first generation and death had occurred about a month previously. During that time, the most likely suspect—a relative with a violent history—had an alibi. With the pupae evidence, Bass could confidently state that maggot activity had started earlier, at a time when the suspect was actually at the scene of the crime. The relative was found guilty of all three murders, and the jury handed down a death sentence. Bass remembers, "I liked that case. The pupal cases nailed him, all right."[53]

Wing Veins, Hairs, and Bristles

After all specimens are collected and larvae are secure in rearing chambers, the process of identification begins. Looking closely at maggots, even dead ones, is often unpleasant, since they have their own unpleasant odor apart from the decaying tissue they feed on. Entomologist Abe Oliver says, "Anytime you put your eyes over a microscope and get that close, it's not going to be pleasant."[54]

Larvae or adult, each specimen is viewed under a microscope so that various identifying structures such as spiracles, mouthparts, eyes, wing veins, hairs, and bristles can be clearly seen. Forensic entomologist David Faulkner explains, "They're very distinctive. Various features that would be like identifying different species of dogs or different sorts of types of dogs. You do it on factors of length, of width, of fur color. These don't have fur, but you do have various structures which are diagnostic, and so you can identify those and determine what ... families you're actually dealing with."[55]

Entomologists know, for instance, that a housefly has a hairy body, a gray striped thorax (part of the body lying behind the head), and a yellow abdomen. Females are larger than males and have more space between their eyes. Blowflies are very large and have blue or green bodies with a metallic sheen. Flesh flies resemble blowflies, but are never metallic colored. Flesh flies can also be differentiated from houseflies by their two sets of bristles above the base of the hind leg and under the base of the wing. Houseflies rarely have both sets.

Answering All the Questions

Not all insects are well-known, and forensic entomologists sometimes collect types that are unfamiliar or apparently out of place. Because these might be important in solving the crime, a specialist is often consulted to help identify them and explain their presence. In the case of crickets crawling on a corpse found in a Hawaiian pineapple field, the expert in charge turned to a graduate student who majored in orthoptera (grasshoppers, crickets, and locusts) at a nearby college for an explanation. The student identified the cricket as a Pacific field cricket (*Teleogryllus oceanicus*), common to Hawaii. He

Entomologists have learned that flesh flies, blowflies, and common house flies have subtle differences.

explained that, because crickets are omnivorous (eating both animals and plants), it was not totally surprising to find them feeding on the body. In the end, the crickets played no part in determining when the victim died, but finding out why they were present was necessary so that they could be ruled out as evidence.

Collecting and identifying insects are just the first steps on the road to determining what the insect evidence means. That next step is more difficult and more subjective because, as forensic entomologist K.C. Kim points out, "It [determining what insect evidence means] has a lot to do with the investigator's experience and intelligence, and that has a lot more to do with art than science."[56] Whether easy or difficult, art or science, analyzing the evidence is a necessary step in the process of discovering when and where the victim died. The bugs have much to tell when a forensic entomologist knows how to read their secrets.

CHAPTER 3

What the Bugs Reveal

Because it is a new field, forensic entomology often plays a small part in criminal investigations. The bug detectives are relative newcomers to the forensic scene, and generally take a back seat to chemists, pathologists, and forensic anthropologists who are consulted first. There are times, however, when insect evidence is the key needed to explain a set of circumstances. Such was the case in the death of a man in Tacoma, Washington, in 1990.

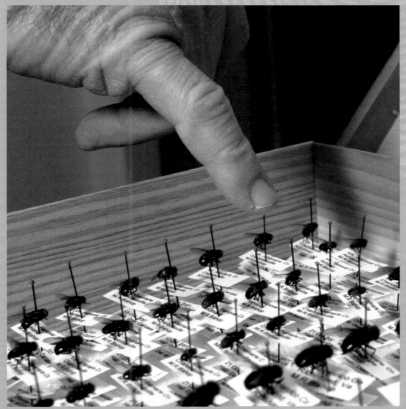

These insect samples are used to match and identify any insects found on or around dead bodies at a crime scene.

49

Becoming a Medical Examiner

Job Description:
Medical examiners investigate sudden and unnatural deaths, perform autopsies, and conduct physical examinations and tests related to any matter of a criminal nature that is being considered by a court or district attorney. If insects are present on the body, medical examiners collect them for further analysis by a forensic entomologist. Medical examiners may be called on to perform forensic medical and pathology consultations, to teach classes in the most current forensic investigative techniques and procedures to law enforcement agencies, and to testify in court to facts and conclusion disclosed by autopsies.

Education:
After four years of college, an aspiring medical examiner must graduate from an accredited four-year medical school, complete a residency program in forensic pathology, and be licensed to practice medicine.

Qualifications:
As a physician, an aspiring medical examiner needs to gain experience in forensic medicine, preferably by serving as an associate or deputy medical examiner. In some cases board certification in forensic pathology is required.

Salary:
$50,000 to $200,000 per year

The incident was a modern-day locked-door mystery. Police found a man's body in the upstairs bedroom of his home where there appeared to have been a struggle. There was blood spatter on the walls, a picture was knocked awry, and the mattress was on the floor. The badly decomposed body was tangled in bedsheets. All doors and windows were locked on the inside. "We had a puzzle on our hands,"[57] said Pierce County sheriff's detective Arthur Anderson.

An autopsy revealed that the victim had died from a bullet wound in the neck. The bullet was found lodged in the wall behind the man's bed. An unused gun lay in a bedside drawer, but its bullets did not match the fatal bullet.

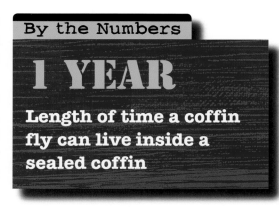

By the Numbers

1 YEAR

Length of time a coffin fly can live inside a sealed coffin

The CSI team collected maggots, pupae cases, and dead flies from on and around the body and sent them to forensic entomologist E. Paul Catts at Washington State University. After looking at everything, Catts determined that the maggots were second generation. Flies had made their way into the house and laid their eggs on the body. Those eggs had hatched and maggots had developed, pupated, and emerged as adwults, leaving the empty pupae cases that Catts had received. The second generation of adults had laid eggs which had hatched into the maggots that Catts also received.

Taking into account temperatures in the locked apartment, Catts estimated that the time since the insects had colonized the body was six weeks. Detectives checked past police records and came upon complaints of shots being fired at a raucous party across the street around that time. They tracked down and interviewed the partygoers, found the shooter, and determined that the bullet in the dead man's wall had come from his gun.

One question remained: How had the man, who had apparently been getting into or out of bed, been killed? Ballistics experts tracked the fatal bullet's path, and discovered that, after it had been fired into the air, it had ricocheted off a metal beam of a nearby garage. On a new course, it had passed through the bathroom window, leaving a small hole in the glass. It then shot across the room, and struck the man in the neck. The disorder in the apartment had been caused by the victim in his death throes. The shooter pleaded guilty to manslaughter and was sentenced to twenty-seven months in prison.

Time of Death

As Catts demonstrated, determining the postmortem interval (PMI)—the time that has elapsed since death—is one of the most important tasks a forensic entomologist is asked to perform. If the PMI is known, police know when the killer was at the scene. They can look for witnesses for that time period. They can try to trace the victim's last movements. Using insect evidence to determine the PMI allows for assessments to be made long after traditional methods—body temperature, livor mortis and rigor mortis—are useless because they have disappeared. In addition, because flies arrive so predictably after death, change so quickly, and leave evidence behind, they allow for more precise determinations than could be made using the above traditional methods.

Forensic entomologists are quick to counter claims that they can use insect evidence to pinpoint time of death, however. Forensic expert William Rodriguez points out, "I will tell you that even as advanced science as we have today, there is no precise, accurate method for determining time since death or that postmortem interval."[58] They can, however, provide estimates of how long insects have colonized the body, and that sometimes be the same as the PMI.

Whether time since colonization is the same as PMI depends on circumstances. If a person is killed in a field and the body is left in the field, flies will lay eggs on the body almost immediately, and time since colonization will be the same as the PMI. If a body is placed in an airtight container where flies cannot get to it for a week and then is moved from the container to an open field with plenty of insects, time since colonization will be one week less than the PMI. If a body is placed in an airtight chamber indefinitely, it is unlikely that insects will ever infest it, and they will be useless in determining PMI.

As a general rule, the more time that elapses between death and discovery of the body, the more that time since colonization becomes an acceptable estimate of the PMI. This is because when a body is found many months or years after death, there is little hope of pinpointing the day or hour that death occurred, even using insect evidence. But if a forensic entomologist can look at pupae evidence and determine that insects colonized the body two years before, investigators are content to say that the PMI is about two years, and will look for corroborating evidence around that time.

Temperature and Time of Death

Forensic entomologists estimate time since colonization by identifying the species present when the body is found. Focusing first on flies, which are the most predictable in their arrival and development, they determine the stage to which the larvae have developed—first, second, or third instar, pre-pupation, or pupation. For instance, if second-instar maggots of bluebottle blowflies are found on a corpse, the entomologist refers to published tables that give development times for that species. He or she notes that adult flies usually arrive at a corpse within

Forensics officers take care to preserve as much of the original crime scene as possible, including focusing on the development of flies around a body, which aids in determining time of death.

By the Numbers

4-8

Number of generations of offspring a fly can produce in one year

an hour of death, that the eggs take an average of twenty-four hours to hatch, and that twenty-four hours are needed to complete the first instar stage. He or she thus estimates that the minimum time since colonization was forty-nine hours: one hour for fly arrival and forty-eight hours for the eggs to hatch and maggots to reach second instar.

Forensic entomologists also take temperatures at a crime scene into account when they determine time since colonization, because temperature dramatically affects insect behavior. Insects are ectotherms, which means that they regulate their body temperature largely by exchanging heat with their surroundings. Their activity and development slows as the air grows cooler. As the air becomes warmer, activity and development speed up.

In order to determine how temperature has affected maggots during their time on a corpse, forensic entomologists must know several temperatures. These include temperature of the body, temperature of the soil, and temperature of the air. They get these by first placing thermocouple probes (similar to thermometers) in several body openings, such as head and abdominal cavity. They place one into the soil. They set up a data logger (an electronic device that records data over time) to record air temperature for a week. They also obtain records of recent temperatures from the nearest weather station for times prior to the body's discovery and for the time of discovery.

Air temperature at the weather station is usually not the same as the temperature at the crime scene. Thus, forensic entomologists compare the temperatures recorded at the weather station and at the crime scene at the time of discovery and make appropriate adjustments. For example, if an average daily temperature at the crime scene was 75°F (24°C), and the average daily temperature at the weather station was 70° (21°C), the entomologist can say that the body was lying in a warmer zone than the weather station prior to its discovery. Knowing that specific temperature difference, temperatures recorded at the weather station prior to the body's discovery can be used to determine temperatures at the crime scene prior to the body's discovery. Those are the temperature conditions under which the insects developed.

Maggot Metabolism

In addition to considering body, soil, and air temperatures, forensic entomologists must take into account the temperature of any maggot masses in the body. The activity of thousands of tiny larvae eating, breathing, and growing can generate a significant amount of heat, particularly if the mass is large. "Maggots

Basic Assumptions

Unless evidence points otherwise, forensic entomologists make several basic assumptions about insects colonizing a corpse. Those assumptions include:

1 Flies are generally inactive at night. Many homicides occur at night, so several hours may pass before flies arrive at the body.

2 Flies will begin depositing their eggs as soon as they arrive at the body.

3 Faunal (animal) succession in and around the corpse follows a predictable pattern.

4 Weather conditions at the death scene generally reflect those recorded at the closest weather station.

5 Air temperature is a major influence on the rate of insect development.

Forensic entomologists take the temperature of any maggot masses found in the body, which can help determine its postmortem interval (the time between death and the discovery of a dead body).

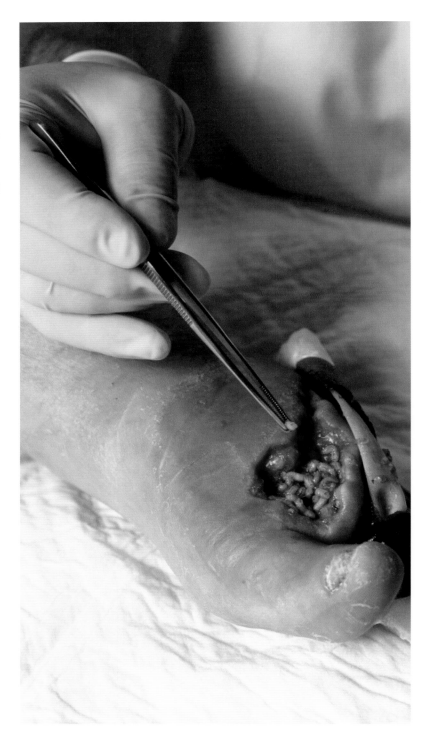

can get trapped in the belly [of a corpse] and literally cook themselves from the metabolic heat they create," says entomology professor Jim Olson. "It can get up to 120 degrees."[59]

Knowing that a large maggot mass can accelerate larval development, entomologists commonly place a thermometer in the center of the mass and record the resulting reading. They cannot assume that each maggot is constantly exposed to the heat in the center, however, because they are constantly moving. Forensic entomologist M. Lee Goff points out, "They seem to circulate through the mass, moving to the inside to feed, and, as their temperatures become dangerously high, moving back to the outside of the mass to cool down and digest. After a period of cooling, they reenter the mass and repeat the cycle. In the process, they spend a good deal of their time at temperatures lower than the temperature at the center of the maggot mass."[60]

Because they have not yet determined exactly how much maggot mass temperature affects maggot development, forensic entomologists must rely on their best estimates in factoring it into their PMI calculations. As a result, two people can come up with two different PMIs for the same body. "They're not wrong, they're just doing things the best way that they know how," says Susan Gruner, a University of Florida researcher who is studying the maggot mass issue. "We have to come up with a standard protocol [procedure] that everybody can use."[61]

Accumulated Degree Hours

After forensic entomologists have determined the species they are working with, the developmental stage of the most mature maggots, and temperatures for the time in question, they are ready to calculate time since colonization. This is done using accumulated degree hours (ADH), a concept that is based on the fact that the speed of insect development is influenced by temperature.

Studies under controlled laboratory conditions have shown that, at a constant given temperature, it takes a set amount of time for insect species to go from one stage of development to another. Tables have been published of these times, so modern entomologists know, for instance, that it always takes blowfly maggots thirty-four hours to hatch and develop to the second instar when the air temperature is 80°F (26.7°C). Any change in temperature, however, will affect the time needed to develop. Cooler temperatures result in a longer period of development and warmer temperatures result in a shorter period. ADH is the product of time and temperature, usually calculated in degrees Celsius. For instance, the ADH for blowfly maggots to reach second instar at a temperature of 26.7°C is 907.8 (34 hours × 26.7°C). If the temperature is lowered to 25.5°C, ADH is still 907.8 because the length of development time at the lower temperature is longer (about 35.6 hours).

With average daily temperatures, the development stage of the maggots, and the ADH for that species under laboratory conditions, forensic entomologists calculate backward to see when flies first laid eggs on the body. Goff emphasizes, "This may not be the actual time of death, but it is the minimum period of time that could have elapsed between death and collection of the insects."[62]

A Real Life Example

An example of how ADH is used to determine time since colonization involves the decomposed body of a woman who was found in her home in Pennsylvania in the 1990s. Neighbors noticed a strong smell of decay coming from the house and broke down the door to find the woman dead on the kitchen floor. There were no signs of violence; she had apparently died of natural causes. When police arrived, they noted that the house was dim and musty, all the doors had been locked, and the windows were tightly covered with glass, screens, and plastic. The shuttered conditions had kept the interior at a fairly constant 72°F (22°C).

Despite the closed doors and windows, flies had been able to get to the body and infest it. With no other way to determine time of death, the medical examiner asked forensic entomologist Stephen W. Bullington to calculate the age of maggots

Calculating Time of Death using Accumulated Degree Hours (ADH): An Example

**Body "X" discovered at home on August 27.
Time of death unknown.**

Temperature of home is 22°C.
Maggots collected from the corpse.

Maggots are moved to laboratory and raised

Maggots are raised in 25°C conditions.
Flies hatch 188 hours later.

ADH in lab calculated as 4700 (188 hours x 25°C)

Fly species identified

Fly species identified as black blowflies.
This species has an ADH of 7403
(from egg to adult).

7403 - 4700 = 2703 ADH from death to discovery of Body "X"

**2703 ADH ÷ 22°C = 123 hours (5 days and 3 hours).
(22°C is the temperature of Body "X's" home at time of death.)**

**According to the calculated ADH, flies estimated to have laid
eggs on Body "X" on August 22.
Death of Body "X" likely occurred on the night of August 21.**

Once a blowfly lays its eggs, as seen here, they will hatch within 24 hours. Unhatched blowfly eggs on a corpse, therefore, indicate a very recent time of death.

found on the corpse. Bullington collected them, preserved half, and took half to the laboratory to be reared to adults. He noted that the temperature in the lab was a constant 77°F (25°C). When the larvae hatched, Bullington identified them as black blowflies (*Phormia regina*). Using reference data on that species' life cycle, he calculated that it took a total of 7,403 ADH for them to go from egg to adult at any constant temperature.

Bullington had collected the maggots from the body at 4 P.M. on August 27, and discovered adult flies hatching from their pupae 188 hours later. The ADH for that time totaled 4,700 (188 hours × 25°C). After subtracting 4,700 from 7,403, 2,703 ADH were left unaccounted for—the time that the maggots had been on the body in the house. The house temperature, 22°C, was divided into the remaining 2,703 ADH, and the final figure was 123 hours (5 days and 3 hours). Counting back five days from August 27, Bullington gave his estimation of when the body was colonized: "The majority of eggs were laid on the body during the daylight hours of 22 Aug. It is likely that death occurred sometime the night before. This conclusion is based on the premise that one or more flies were either already present in the house, or that they had unimpeded access to the kitchen through the garage. I think one or the other of these possibilities is extremely likely."[63]

Was the Body Moved?

In addition to determining time since colonization, forensic entomologists can sometimes answer other questions relating to a crime. The most common is whether a body has been moved from one locale to another after death.

As with almost all animals, insect species have certain environments they prefer, whether that is a certain type of vegetation, a certain elevation, or a certain geographic locale. For instance, bluebottle blowflies will breed indoors while greenbottle blowflies seldom do. If investigators find insect evidence on a corpse that seems to be out of place, they suspect that the body was originally in a different locale. Forensic entomologist Robert Kimsey explains: "You might find a corpse in an open field, its clothes heavily infested with cockroaches. Well, domestic cockroaches are simply never found in random ecosystems. They're associated only with human beings and then generally only where the domicile [home] is very heavily infested. Chances are that corpse became a corpse in an infested domicile and was later dumped in an open field."[64]

Forensic entomologists knew they were not looking at an original crime scene when the body of a murdered woman was found in a sugarcane field in Hawaii. The presence of maggots of an uncommon urban species of fly, *Synthesionyia nudiseta*, told them that the body had been in a city or suburb before being placed in the field. In addition, the urban maggots had been developing for five days, while other maggot species on the body were only at a three-day stage. When the victim was identified, police learned that she had been killed in a Honolulu apartment during a drug deal gone wrong. With an unexpected corpse on their hands, the killers had panicked, hidden it in the apartment for two days, and then disposed of it in the field.

Establishing Identity

At times, forensic entomologists know a body has been moved because they find insect evidence at a scene and nothing else. Forensic entomologist Jeffrey Wells explains, "Sometimes we come upon a site where we suspect there might have been a body—but when we get there, there's no body, just a bunch of larvae lying around. ... Sometimes the killer waits a while before hauling off a corpse and burying it someplace. When a body is moved—from the trunk of a car, a basement, the woods—some of the maggots may fall off."[65]

Even without the body, the insects can sometimes provide the identity of the victim. By analyzing the DNA (genetic

Pubic lice feed on the blood of their host, and blood contains the host's DNA. Forensic entomologists have used the DNA found in insects' digestive tracts to identify criminal suspects.

Maggot Milkshake

Forensic entomologists use creative techniques to help determine how victims die. In his article, "VCU Forensic Science Techniques Uses Bugs to Help Crack Crimes," journalist Mike Frontiero explains:

When police discover a badly decomposed body, it's hard to tell how the person died, leaving many crimes unsolved. Now, researchers at Virginia Commonwealth University [(VCU)] are testing a concoction of flesh-eating bugs that could provide the break police need to determine how and when the person died. "What's found in the bugs could very much help steer a death investigation in the right direction," said Jennifer S. Strano, a forensic investigator with the Henrico County Police Department in Virginia.

Maggots recovered from a victim's body are being tested for clues by grinding them up in a blender to separate toxins that the bugs consumed on the body. Samples of the mixture are placed in test tubes, where a special chemical is added to help the toxins float to the top, where they can be removed for analysis. The researchers have coined the mixture "The Maggot Milkshake." "You are what you eat. So if the body had taken any type of drugs prior to death, and the maggots are eating on that body, then the drugs are going to wind up in the maggots," says lead researcher and VCU toxicology graduate student Michelle R. Peace.

Mike Frontiero, "VCU Forensic Science Techniques Uses Bugs to Help Crack Crimes," VCU News Center, May 29, 2002. www.news.vcu.edu/news.aspx?v=detail&nid=642.

material unique to each human being) in blood and tissue that maggots have previously consumed, forensic entomologists have been able to help police develop a profile that matches a missing person.

DNA found in insects has led to the identification of perpetrators, too. In the best-known case, a pubic louse (a parasitic insect which spends its entire life on human hair and feeds exclusively on blood) was found during the examination of a rape victim. She had not been previously infested. Police guessed that the insect had come from the attacker during his assault and took it to an entomologist for analysis. Human blood from its gut (primitive digestive tract) was recovered, a DNA profile was created, and a suspect identified. The man was convicted in part based on the insect evidence.

Cause of Death

There are times when forensic entomologists help determine cause of death by analyzing the contents of the maggots' guts as well as their tissues, larval skins, and pupal casings. The presence of drugs including cocaine, methamphetamines, and antidepressants is easily detected and can help investigators determine if the victim died of an overdose. Crime novelist and forensic expert Kathy Reichs explains, "You are what you eat—so if maggots have been feeding on the body of someone who was a chronic drug user, … you're probably going to pick that up in the gut of the maggot."[66]

Maggots can also be analyzed for gunshot residue, which they ingest when they eat the flesh around bullet wounds. Like drugs, the residue remains in their tissues, skins, and pupa cases long after the corpse has become skeletonized. Australian forensic entomologist Ian Dadour says, "You can actually extract gunshot residue from spent pupal cases, and they hang around crime scenes for up to two years."[67]

In certain instances, forensic entomologists can get clues about the cause of death by the location of maggots on a corpse. In addition to infesting body openings, flies are drawn to wounds, so when an area of advance decomposition—known as differential decomposition—is seen on the body, experts know that a victim has been injured there and may have died from the wounds.

Differential decomposition reopened the case of eighteen-year-old Lisa Rinker, who was murdered in 1984. A community search located her body almost a week after she went missing. The corpse was badly decomposed and there was no evidence to lead to a suspect, so she was buried and no one was charged with a crime. Sometime later, however, police asked Rodriguez to look at photos of the crime scene. From the unusually large amount of insect activity and decomposition on Lisa's chest and abdomen, Rodriguez suspected that she had sustained several wounds in those areas. Insect activity on her hands also suggested defense wounds, sustained when she attempted to defend herself against attack. The body was exhumed and the skeleton was examined for trauma. As expected, seven knife marks were found on the rib bones. The case was reclassified as a homicide, but police were never able to identify Lisa's killer.

Neglect and Abuse

In addition to providing clues about cause of death, insects are powerful indicators of neglect and abuse. People who are too weak to move and are poorly cared for develop sores caused by pressure, lack of circulation, and filth. Flies are drawn to these conditions and can infest the wounds even when the victims are alive. For instance, maggots have been found on elderly nursing home residents who have been left in close contact with fecal and urine-soiled clothes or bedding. Goff writes, "The maggots document the duration of the neglect. If a bedridden person is bathed every day, as the caretakers in these cases claimed, it is extremely difficult to explain the presence of 5-day-old maggots in the sore."[68]

Neglected infants and small children are also at risk for maggot infestation. In Hawaii in 1990, for example, a female

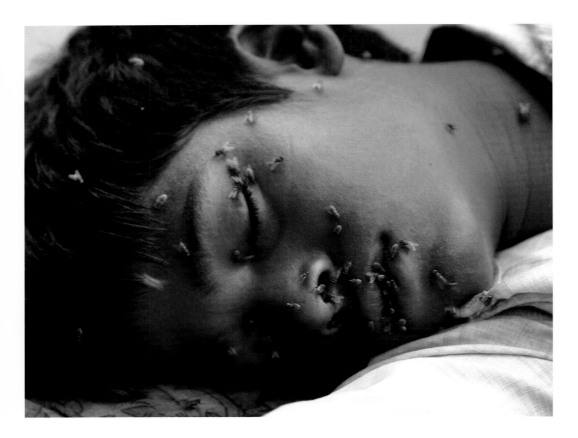

When individuals are too weak to move and/or are poorly cared for, they can develop sores that flies are drawn to and infest, even when the victims are alive.

infant was found close to death near a lake on the island of Oahu. She was dehydrated, bruised, and had maggots in her diaper. "They [the police] were trying to determine how long the child had been lying there. ... She was near death. ... She was quiet enough that flies had been attracted,"[69] stated Goff, who was called to evaluate the case.

In order to determine when the baby had been left by the lake, Goff studied the maggots and decided that they had been deposited at least twenty-seven hours earlier. When the child's mother was identified, she claimed that the baby had been kidnapped, but police proved otherwise. The mother was charged with and found guilty of attempted murder.

Insect evidence has many applications, and its analysis has great potential. A single mistake, such as the misidentification of a species or the miscalculation of a development period can yield incorrect results, however. As a consequence, a guilty person might get away with murder, or an innocent one might be sent to jail. Thus, forensic entomologists continue to push the boundaries of what they know to make their findings as accurate as possible. Goff says, "I do not take this responsibility lightly and am careful to analyze and reanalyze my data. ...When someone's life is at stake, all the enthusiasm in the world is a poor substitute for accuracy."[70]

Chapter 4

What Affects the Bugs

As forensic entomologists gain more experience in crime solving, they become increasingly aware that insects are very sensitive to their environment. Any number of things ranging from wind to blankets to drugs can and does affect their activity and development. It seems reasonable that every variable needs to be taken into account in order to get the most accurate PMI, particularly when the results can be scrutinized in court. Forensic entomologist Carl Olson notes, "The legal profession is very nit-picky, and if you don't have the ability to say, 'Yeah, we've looked at this sort of situation,' then they'll discount you."[71]

As a result, forensic entomologists concentrate on the crime scene microclimate—conditions on, under, and within a few yards of the body—and how it affects the insects. They consider the locations of nearby bushes, streams, highways, and anything else that might affect temperature, humidity, access to the body, and/or the health of the insects. Ignoring these factors can result in mistaken analyses. Taking them into account at the very least helps eliminate confusion, as Goff proved in 1984.

That year, the bug expert was asked to estimate the PMI of a female whose insect-covered corpse had been found on the grounds of an abandoned brewery. Goff was given the insects to analyze, and they seemed to indicate two different times of colonization. Puzzled, he visited the crime scene and discovered that the corpse had, in effect, been decomposing in a unique microclimate. It had been lying across a shallow drainage ditch with its back partway in water, so the flesh on the back had stayed moist. Maggots had been able to feed longer there than they would have on a dry body. The front of the body, on the other hand, had been in the sun. Maggots had come and gone

Proper Adjustments

As forensic entomologist M. Lee Goff explains in his book, A Fly for the Prosecution, *when inexperienced or sloppy forensic entomologists fail to take the environment into account in analyzing insect activity, their conclusions can be wrong:*

Data from a desert cannot properly be applied to a corpse found in a city or a pine forest without proper adjustments. I have been made aware of at least one instance where my data from Hawaii were applied to a case in Florida without adequate consideration of differences in either geography or environmental conditions. My data, derived from a decomposition study conducted in a lush rain forest on the island of Oahu, were applied to a corpse found on a nearly barren Florida sandbar. Aside from the obvious problems with that comparison, the fact that a hurricane had moved through the area during the period in question was not considered significant by the person providing the estimate of the postmortem interval. Needless to say, the estimated time since death bore no resemblance to the time that had really elapsed.

M. Lee Goff, *A Fly for the Prosecution: How Insect Evidence Helps Solve Crimes.* Cambridge, MA: Harvard University Press, 2000, p. 33.

more quickly, making way for hide beetles and other species. By taking the variables into consideration, Goff decided that insect activity on the front of the corpse gave the most accurate information. He remembers, "In time, a suspect was identified. … In late September 1985, I testified as to the probable time of death during a murder trial in the First Circuit Court in Honolulu. The suspect was convicted of second degree murder and the major witnesses were flies."[72]

Decomposition Studies

Forensic entomologists noticed as early as the 1980s that microclimates affected the insects, but they had no way of knowing exactly how to factor the many variables into their calculation of time of colonization. To gain more knowledge, they set up controlled decomposition studies, during which they observed and

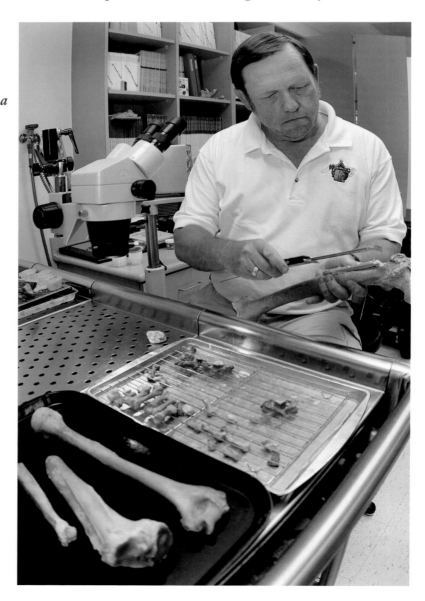

John Williams, director of the Human Identification Lab at Western Carolina University, examines a human femur in 2006. This university houses only the second so-called "body farm" in the United States, where studies are conducted on human decomposition.

recorded differences in the rate of decay and insect development under a predetermined set of conditions.

Using human bodies in these studies was impractical in most cases due to legal and public opposition. Exceptions were the Anthropology Research Facility (also known as the Body Farm) at the University of Tennessee in Knoxville and the Western Carolina Human Identification Laboratory at Western Carolina University, Cullowhee, North Carolina. As of 2008, a third locale was in the planning stages at the Texas State University Forensic Research Facility at San Marcos.

As an alternative to human bodies, many forensic entomologists chose 50-pound (23kg) domestic pigs as subjects for their studies. These animals' muscle to fat ratio, decay rate, and insect activity patterns closely mimic human ones. The pigs were practical to use for other reasons, too, as Goff points out: "[The subjects of our studies] must be readily available in large numbers so that studies can be replicated. Also the animal must be relatively cheap to obtain because funds are truly limited. Finally, it must be an animal whose carcass will not unduly upset any members of the community who may encounter an experiment in progress while on an afternoon walk or weekend hike."[73]

Three Pigs

Using humanely killed animals, decomposition studies took place in various geographic locations across the United States and around the world. The studies allowed forensic entomologists to build a database of insects that were native to their locale as well as study an infinite number of variables. Carcasses were placed in surroundings similar to those where human corpses were often found—in landfills, along roads in remote areas, or in heavily wooded, brushy areas. They were studied in real situations—clothed in cast-off garments, wrapped in blankets, buried, frozen, or burned. They were laid out on cement slabs, hung in trees, or covered with leaves.

For each individual study, three newly killed animals were placed about 55 feet (17m) apart early in the morning before fly activity began. Each was protected from large scavengers by mesh cages that were open at the bottom. One carcass was the control, left untouched for the duration of the study. One was used to determine the rate of tissue removal during decomposition. It was placed on the ground on a wire mesh screen attached to a scale so that weight loss could be measured. The third was used for sampling the insects, which were collected, taken to the lab, and analyzed. The carcasses were visited at predetermined intervals for at least three weeks, with temperatures and photographs taken, insects collected, and observations recorded at each visit.

As questions were answered, new ones rose to take their place, so the studies have become a continuing part of forensic entomology work. Forensic entomologist Amoret Brandt describes a study she instituted in 2004: "We were asked to visit a crime scene to search for puparial cases. The problem was that the crime was two years old, and no research has been done on how long empty puparial cases remain intact in the soil. So I started a study where I buried a large number of empty … cases and over a period of three years I dig them up. The results should be able to tell us the rate at which the puparial cases degrade over time. … So next time we're faced with an 'old' crime, we'll be better able to help."[74]

Sun, Shade, Humidity, and Wind

Because temperature is a key component in insect development, many decomposition studies have focused on variables that affect temperature. Even when the results were not surprising, the studies allowed differences in insect activity under specific conditions to be documented and compared. Researchers noted that shady environments are usually cooler than sunnier ones, so insects develop slower there. In sunny locales, especially in the summer,

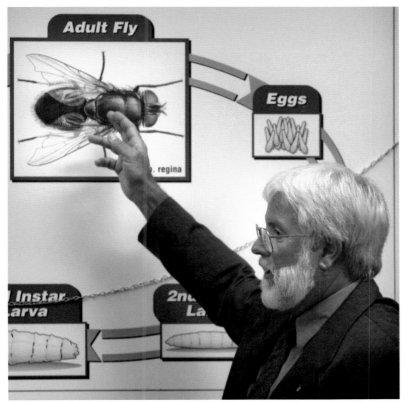

Forensic scientist Dr. M. Lee Goff testifies during the David Westerfield murder trial in 2002.

both the body and the ground absorb and hold heat. This absorbed warmth allows maggot activity to continue into the night when cooler air temperatures would normally slow activity.

Researchers also studied how humidity combined with warm temperatures increased insect numbers and activity. Jungles with their many and various insect species illustrate this, and bodies placed there were found to completely decompose in as little as eighteen days. On the other hand, too much moisture kept some insects away. Bodies placed in very wet locales never dried enough to attract hide beetles, hister beetles, and others that normally colonize the body during the postdecay phase.

While humid conditions speed up decomposition, arid conditions dramatically slow the arrival of flies. This is because when bodies dry, they frequently become mummified. Moisture decreases, the skin becomes tough, and flies are not attracted

The Body Farm

The Forensic Anthropology Center at the University of Tennessee was founded by renowned forensic anthropologist William Bass. In their article, "Pastoral Putrefaction Down on the Body Farm," journalists Michele Dula Baum and Toria Tolley explain the facility's origins:

Nearly everything known about the science of human decomposition comes from one place—forensic anthropologist William Bass' Body Farm. On three acres surrounded by razor-wire and a wooden fence near the University of Tennessee Medical Center, about 40 bodies rot away at any given time. They're stuffed into car trunks, left lying in the sun or shade, buried in shallow graves, covered with brush or submerged in ponds. ...

"It was a need-to-know thing," said Bass, explaining the origins of the Body Farm. For 11 years as a forensic anthropologist in Kansas, Bass had dealt with skeletal remains. ... Once he joined the University of Tennessee faculty, "half of the first 10 cases I got were maggot-covered bodies," he remembered. "And people (detectives) don't ask you 'Who is that,' they ask 'How long have they been there?'"

At the time, "there was nothing much in the literature," Bass realized. "So I asked the dean if I could have a small piece of land to put bodies on. That was the beginning of what has been 29 years of trying to figure out what happens to people. I think all we've done is scratch the surface."

Michele Dula Baum and Toria Tolley, "Pastoral Putrefaction Down on the Body Farm," HBO, 2008. www.hbo.com/autopsy/forensic/the_body_farm.html.

to lay their eggs. Even if maggots infest a drying corpse, they soon find it too tough to chew and stop their activity earlier than they might otherwise. Insects such as beetles that prefer dry conditions, however, arrive earlier than otherwise expected and remain for longer periods of time.

Although few studies have yet focused on the specific effects of wind, workers in the field note that it can decrease the fly population. They assume this is because it disperses odors and makes it difficult for insects to settle. Also, it is drying and can bring about mummification. In the Danielle van Dam case of 2002 in San Diego, California, forensic entomologists postulated that Santa Ana winds—strong, extremely dry offshore winds that periodically sweep through Southern California—had caused Danielle's body to dry quickly, discouraging insect colonization.

Light, Dark, Highs, and Lows

In addition to heat, humidity, and wind, forensic entomologists studied the effects of the seasons, with their variations in temperature, weather, and daylight hours. They knew from experience that locales with very cold winters, for instance, had virtually no insect activity because insects become dormant if air temperature drops. They learned however, that blowflies are inactive below about 54°F (12°C) and fly larvae stop developing around 50°F (10°C). Thus, if a body is deposited outdoors in Minnesota in December, there will be no evidence of insect activity until spring.

Just as cold temperatures shut down insect activity, so do bad-weather days. Researchers found that flies are extremely sensitive to changes in light, so that even during periods that are warm enough for activity, weather events such as clouds, rain, and fog will bring all activity to a virtual standstill.

Flies are most active during summer days due to the abundance of heat and light, but studies showed that even on these days, there are peak periods of activity. Not surprisingly, these come in mid-afternoon when temperatures are

highest. At night, on the other hand, flies are inactive, although some insect experts debate that conclusion. In one Indiana study, forensic entomologist Neal Haskell placed pigs outside at night and saw no flies, even during warm, midsummer conditions with a full moon illuminating the landscape. Forensic entomologists Bernard Greenberg and M. Lee Goff, on the other hand, testify to the fact that they have seen flies active around corpses both in early-morning light and in late-night darkness. Goff states: "Although blow flies do not usually fly or seek food or egg-laying sites at night, if the temperatures remain above the threshold required for activity and a suitable food source is dumped nearby, they can become active and lay eggs."[75] More studies are necessary to better understand the variables that may come into play in dark conditions.

Access to the Body

While some forensic entomologists focused on the effects of daylight versus darkness and summer versus winter, others looked at variables that delay or prevent insect access to a corpse. They assumed that clothing would be one hindering factor, but in fact, the opposite proved true. Studies revealed that egg-laying time is extended and maggot masses appear sooner and grow larger if a corpse is clothed. This is because clothing is loose, yet absorbs and holds moisture such as blood and body fluids, all of which are attractive to flies. On the other hand, clothing slows the arrival of beetles that prefer the corpse to be dry.

Covering or concealing a body completely does delay insect colonization, however. If a body is wrapped in a tarp or shut it in a closet, for example, the odor of decay cannot escape into the air as fast, so flies are not alerted to the body's presence. Once the flies arrive, they must make their way to the flesh.

Even the tiniest opening—a small drainage hole in a car's spare tire well or a slightly loose twist tie on a garbage bag—affords them passage, but the process takes time.

On at least one occasion, flies could not access a concealed body despite time and their best efforts. In Indiana, thousands of blowflies were seen swarming above a junk pile in a rural community, and when police investigated, they found that a body had been thrown down an open well. The well had then been filled with tires, rocks, and other debris, but the smell of decay had been strong enough to reach the surface. When the corpse was finally recovered, no insect activity was found on it because the intervening material had been too deep and compact to allow them to reach it.

Decomposition studies not only substantiated observations that coverings and concealment slowed insect arrival, but they also provided answers for how long it took insects to get past various coverings. For instance, if a body was loosely wrapped,

A cadaver dog (dogs trained to locate dead bodies) locates a clothed body in a remote wooded area. Insect activity on a corpse can be altered depending on whether a corpse is clothed or otherwise covered up.

colonization was delayed by only an hour or two. If it was wrapped tightly in several blankets, the delay was over two days. And when the body was buried, even a thin layer of soil slowed blowfly colonization by a week. If flies managed to deposit their eggs on the corpse before burial, however, larvae survived and sometimes reproduced underground.

"A Little Strange"

Almost all decomposition studies are well-planned research projects, but a few are impromptu to get a quick answer to an urgent question. Goff, for instance, was asked to testify regarding the PMI in a case where the body of a woman was found wrapped tightly in layers of fabric and bound with Ace bandages. She had been missing thirteen days, but insects appeared to have been active only ten and a half days. Goff believed that the two and a half day difference could be accounted for by insects having to make their way through the coverings, but he could not be sure. Thus, he obtained a pig carcass and placed

An entomologist works with fly samples found on a corpse.

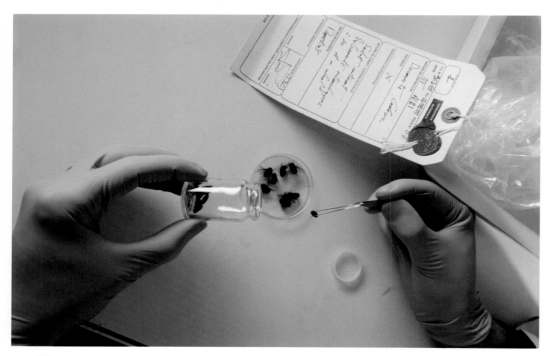

Fly Tracks

Fly artifacts—marks left by flies—are one factor that forensic entomologists and crime scene investigators are only beginning to take into account when they visit a death scene. In some cases, hundreds of tiny, irregular bloodstains are found on lamp shades, blinds, ceilings, and even on the victim. These marks look like blood spatter caused by beatings or gunshots and suggest that a struggle took place. When investigators try to reconstruct the source of the blows, however, the results are confusing and contradictory.

To find answers, forensic entomologist Mark Benecke and investigator Larry Barksdale studied the problem. They determined that many of the stains were made by flies that visited the body. Landing on the victim, the insects' tiny feet picked up blood that they then tracked onto other surfaces. They also ingested blood from the victim and then, as is their habit, regurgitated it onto nearby surfaces for later consumption.

As a result of their studies, Benecke and Barksdale believe that fly activity should be considered at all crime scenes, and that investigators should learn to tell the difference between fly tracks and criminal activity. They state, "Forensic scientists, crime scene technicians and investigators may encounter blood spatter at a scene which may be pure or a mixture of fly artifacts and human bloodstains. It is important to be able to make an informed identification, or at least advanced documentation of such stains."

Mark Benecke and Larry Barksdale, "Distinction of Bloodstain Patterns from Fly Artifacts," *Forensic Science International*, 2003, pp. 152–159.

it in a locale similar to where the murder had taken place—in this case, his own backyard. He wrapped the animal to simulate the human corpse, covered it with a mesh cage to protect it from his pets, and observed it every four hours for the next

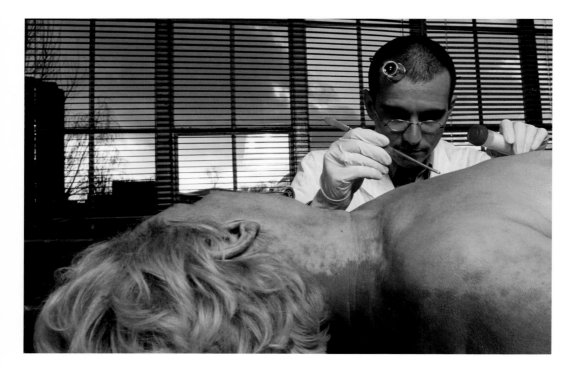

Forensic entomologist Mark Benecke performs a post-mortem.

thirteen hours. He remembers, "My neighbors started to think I was a little strange, [but] we nailed the time and the guy [the woman's husband] was convicted of murder."[76]

In a similar situation that involved forensic entomologist David Faulkner, eighteen-year-old Offord Rollins IV was charged with the murder of his seventeen-year-old girlfriend on August 2, 1991. Her corpse had been found late that same night in a nearby field. The prosecutor claimed that Rollins had committed the crime about 1:30 P.M. that same day.

When Faulkner looked at the autopsy report and crime scene photos, he expected to see flies and maggots on the corpse. August 2 had been warm, and the body had allegedly been outside all afternoon. No insect activity was visible, however. To test if there were flies in the field, Faulkner placed the carcass of a small pig in the exact spot where the victim's body had been. Flies arrived within thirty minutes, and by midnight, the body was covered with maggots. The forensic entomologist could draw only one conclusion—the body had not been in the field during the afternoon hours. It had been placed there after dark when the flies were inactive.

Rollins had been with friends continuously after 2:00 P.M. on August 2, but neither his alibi nor Faulkner's testimony convinced the jury, and he was convicted. After three years in prison, however, he won a retrial with the help of Faulkner's fly evidence, and he was freed in 1996.

Hung and Burned

The results of decomposition studies do not usually surprise researchers, but those carried out using hanged and burned pig carcasses did produce unexpected results. Forensic entomologists knew from observation that bodies found hanging usually had less than expected insect activity. They did not understand why until they watched developments during a study that suspended a pig carcass in the air. Flies arrived and laid their eggs, and maggots hatched on schedule and formed masses on both the control carcass on the ground and on the one in the air, but then the pattern of activity changed. As maggots fed and migrated in and out of the mass on the hanging carcass, they had nothing to hold onto, and many fell to the ground. Once there, they could not get back up and continue eating. That slowed decomposition significantly. Goff also notes: "The hanging pig was also more exposed to the effects of wind and air, and its tissues dried out more rapidly than those of the ground pig. Consequently the hanging pig could not be used as food by the maggots as long as the ground pig."[77]

A study that involved burning a carcass surprised researchers, too. They had expected that charred remains would be so dry and hard that flies would not be attracted to it. In studies, however, they found just the opposite to be true. Burning produced odors that caused insects to arrive more quickly than expected. In some cases, flies landed on one part of the carcass while the other part was still in flames. In addition, they not only laid eggs in the natural body openings, but they also deposited eggs on many small cracks in the skin caused by the fire. Overall results showed that decomposition and insect activity was uniformly four days ahead of the control through-out the burn studies.

The accuracy of research on a burned body was demon-strated in Taiwan in 2007. A badly burned female corpse was found a short distance from where decomposition studies were being carried out. Researchers were able to compare maggot development on the corpse to maggot development on a burned pig carcass, and estimated that the corpse had been incinerated about fifty hours previously. After the murderer was arrested, police learned that the PMI was actually forty-six hours, a close match to the researcher's estimation.

Drugs and Chemicals

When estimating time since colonization and PMI, bug experts not only consider factors that affect temperature and access to the body. They also study substances that affect insect physiology—how their bodies function. These substances could be pesticides that kill off an insect population, or poisons ingested by the victim that make the corpse unattractive to the insects. More often, they are drugs in the victim's body that affect insect growth after they feed on body tissues.

Goff is just one of several forensic entomologists to study the effects of drugs on insect development. He found that flies fed cocaine-laced liver had eggs that developed at a normal rate, but early instar stages developed more rapidly than would be expected. During late third-instar stage, development returned to normal. Other studies showed that heroin slowed blowfly maggot growth, although it did not appear to affect cheese skipper maggots at all. Maggots fed tissue infused with phen-cyclidine, commonly known as PCP, developed at a normal rate, but many of them died during the pupal stage.

A case investigated by forensic entomologist E. Paul Catts illustrates how important it is for forensic entomologists to consider drugs when making their determinations. In the late 1980s, the medical examiner in Spokane, Washington, sent Catts maggots from the corpse of a woman who had been

Certain substances found in victims' bodies have an effect on insect growth after they feed on body tissues. Cocaine, for example, causes some types of maggots to grow at an accelerated rate.

stabbed. Her body had been found in the woods, and the PMI needed to be determined. Catts identified most of the maggots on the body as being at the seven-day stage. There were a few exceptions—taken from the region of the nose—that were twice as large as the others, suggesting they had been developing for three weeks. Catts knew that was unlikely because the victim had allegedly been seen alive two weeks before.

In considering the variables that could produce such large maggots, Catts thought of the possibility of drugs. He spoke with his colleague, Goff, who was carrying out cocaine studies at the time, and learned that cocaine caused maggots to grow at an accelerated rate. Catts asked the Spokane medical examiner if the victim had been a drug user and learned that she had been seen snorting cocaine shortly before she disappeared. That explained the mystery: The maggots had fed in the nasal area where a high level of cocaine caused them to develop faster than the others. Goff notes, "[We came up with a] developmental time for the largest maggots of approximately 7 days, the same as for the most numerous maggots present on the corpse." [78]

Overgrown maggots, burned corpses, and dead pigs in one's backyard are routine for forensic entomologists. Testifying in court is a test of their patience and perspective, however. When they testify, forensic entomologists must justify their work to lawyers and juries who are ignorant of insect behavior. They must submit to interrogation that seems designed to make them appear to be liars or fools. They must remain clear headed and unflustered even after hours on the witness stand. They do all that solely for the sake of justice, the victims, and their own self-respect. As forensic entomologist Joe Keiper says, "You have to treat people with respect, you have to become a little detached—put your game face on and act like a professional." [79]

CHAPTER 5

Insects in Court

As recognized authorities on insects and crime, forensic entomologists are often called as expert witnesses in court. This seldom happened prior to the 1990s, because their field was new and unappreciated. When they were called, however, their opinions were accepted without question, primarily because attorneys knew too little to challenge them. Forensic entomologist M. Lee Goff notes, "For the first few trials where I testified, … I gave a brief explanation of forensic entomology, told how the evidence had been collected and analyzed, and then presented my interpretations of the evidence. No alternate analysis or interpretation of the evidence was given to the jury."[80]

All that changed as police and lawyers became more aware of what the insects could prove. Today, both prosecution and defense attorneys recruit their own forensic entomologists to present testimony and counter the opposition in court. "A court case with a single entomologist is a thing of the past,"[81] says forensic entomologist Jason Byrd, who notes that lawyers have also become skilled in attacking the credibility of the experts. They insist on short "yes" or "no" answers to complex questions and construct their questions to get the answers they desire. The result is frustrating and often unsettling, as Goff points out: "[The] process sometimes reminds me of a board game where the rules are incidental to the action on the board. Science tends to take a backseat to the legal manipulations, and it frequently requires a major effort to keep the focus of testimony on the problem being addressed."[82]

Expert Witnesses

Due to the adversarial nature of a trial, forensic entomologists have come to realize that almost anything they say as an expert witness will be open to questioning. Thus, they begin

Flies and Freedom

Insect evidence was often dismissed by courts in the 1980s. In the article "Lord of the Flies" Alex Lange illustrates how flies helped free an innocent man ten years after he was convicted of murder. Lange says:

In 1984, a man fishing in a rural Pennsylvania river spotted what he thought was a dead pig in a cardboard box. As he approached it, he discovered to his horror that it wasn't a pig but the limbless and headless torso of a woman. After the police investigated the area, the victim's remains were taken to the county medical examiner. During the autopsy several maggots were extracted from the wound, photographed and cataloged. But the evidence was never introduced in the trial, and the suspected killer, a man named Donald Ruby, was convicted and sentenced to time in prison.

Almost a decade later, Ruby was granted a new trial, the maggot evidence was allowed, and [forensic entomologists Robert] Hall and [Neal] Haskell were asked to testify. Because the maggot eggs found on the body were unhatched, the two determined that the minimum time interval (3 days) in which the victim's torso could have been dumped at the riverbank was consistent with Ruby's alibi, and he was exonerated.

Alex Lange, "Lord of the Flies," *Vox Magazine*, August 2, 2007. www.voxmagazine.com/stories/2007/08/02/lord-flies.

preparing for a possible visit to court from the moment they receive evidence.

They keep complete records of everything so they can substantiate their testimony. They try to account for every variable that could affect their conclusions. They think carefully about what they are going to say. Goff says, "I have encountered many entomologists who began a case with naïve enthusiasm, not realizing that they would ultimately be required to present their results during a trial. … [They] offered opinions and speculations that were not supported by the evidence. … By the time I entered these cases, the entomologists had become painfully aware of their mistakes."[83]

The trial often takes place months or years after the investigation, so before going to court, forensic entomologists review the facts and all the evidence they have collected so they can speak with confidence. They meet with the legal team that requested their services and learn what aspects of the evidence are most significant. Even though they are testifying for either the prosecution or the defense, however, they always try to provide an honest, unbiased analysis of the evidence. Forensic

During the David Westerfield murder trial in 2002, attorney Steven Feldman (left) questions Dr. M. Lee Goff (right), the chairman of the forensic science department at Chaminade University of Honolulu.

expert Bill Bass says, "My role in a case was not to serve the prosecutor or the defendant; my role—my only role—was to speak for the victim by uncovering the truth."[84]

On the Stand

Once on the witness stand, forensic entomologists must present their credentials to convince the judge and the jury that they are qualified to speak as an expert. At the prompting of the attorney, they then present basic information about life cycles and development stages of flies and beetles so that the jury can understand subsequent testimony. "Every time I've been in a court, I've had to take the judge and the jury through the life cycle of a fly,"[85] says Australian entomologist Beryl Morris.

Proceeding on to give testimony, they aim to explain their findings as clearly as possible. They try to avoid the jargon of their profession while not talking down to their audience. They avoid referring to insects solely by their Latin names and briefly define confusing terms such as "accumulated degree days," and "faunal succession." Inevitably they have to explain why they came to their conclusions, however, and this usually involves discussions of time, temperature, and mathematical calculations, which can be tedious and confusing. Opposition attorneys encourage both conditions to undercut the experts' standing with the jury. Goff recalls, "During one trial, I spent well over an hour on the stand using a hand calculator to redo several calculations. The defense attorney had his calculator and I had mine. We entered the same figures and performed the same calculations while the jury became increasingly stupefied and restless."[86]

In order to keep the jury's attention and help the members understand the issues, forensic entomologists present visual representations to reinforce

By the Numbers

350,000

Number of known species of beetles worldwide

their statements. These can include graphs, maps, and photos of insects and maggots on the victim's body. The latter are compelling, but can be deeply disturbing as well. Journalist Charles Slack says, "The slides of half-eaten faces and crawling bowels get the message across,"[87] but proceedings sometimes have to halt if someone becomes queasy or if the defense argues that the photos are too prejudicial to use.

Preparing for a Challenge

Even presenting the facts and conclusions clearly and carefully does not exempt forensic entomologists from challenges, and their sternest critics are their own colleagues who have been brought in to testify for the other side. In the case of Kevin Neal, charged with murdering his two stepchildren in Ohio in the summer of 1997, forensic entomologist Martin Hall flatly contradicted forensic entomologist Neal Haskell, who stated that the children had died before mid-July. Haskell based his

Dr. Neal Haskell, an expert on the blowfly life cycle, uses his expertise to help solve murder cases.

A Developing Field

As science and technology progress, forensic entomologists look for more and better ways to apply insect evidence to crime solving. For instance, at Rhodes University in South Africa in 2008, entomologist and researcher Angela Brownes is working on a computer program known as Identifly, which she believes will prove significant in criminal investigations. Identifly is a software package that allows the user to identify insects based on their shape and structure. The program is user-friendly in that it has interactive keys and illustrations to make identification easier. When a corpse is discovered, an investigator can compare certain characters of insects found on that corpse with the illustrations on the keys. Once the species and its life history are known, the investigator will be able to determine its growth rate, its survival conditions, and the amount of time the insects have been present on the corpse. The program will hopefully increase accuracy and speed in criminal investigations.

conclusion on the fact that he had found evidence of blowfly infestation on the bodies, but had seen no trace of secondary screwworm flies (*Cochliomyia macellaria*), which are common in Ohio in mid to late summer. He explained that screwworm flies died off in the winter. "It has to repopulate every spring as it warms up,"[88] he said at the trial. Neal was alleged to have killed his stepchildren about the time they disappeared on July 9. Haskell pointed out that the absence of the secondary screwworm larvae on the bodies meant that the children had been killed before screwworm flies were present to colonize the bodies.

Hall, who testified for the defense, disagreed with Haskell. He was convinced that the arrival of the secondary screwworm was too variable to base conclusions on. Temperatures influenced when the fly returned to Ohio. The rate that it repopulated the area was variable too. "From my analysis of this, I don't see how a forensic entomologist could be as precise as is reflected in Dr. Haskell's report,"[89] he stated bluntly.

By the Numbers

300 MILLION

Number of years insects have existed

Hall eliminated the secondary screwworm from his calculations, concentrating instead on the development stages of other flies found on the bodies. Those led him to conclude that colonization was much later than Haskell estimated, sometime around mid-September. At that time, Neal had been in prison on an unrelated charge. Despite the disagreement between insect experts, the jury found Neal guilty of the murders and sentenced him to life in prison.

High-Profile Dispute

One of the most high-profile disputes over insect evidence took place during the murder trial of David Westerfield, accused of kidnapping and murdering seven-year-old Danielle van Dam. Danielle disappeared from her home in San Diego, California, on the night of February 1, 2002. Specks of her blood were found on Westerfield's clothing and in his motor home, and he was arrested on February 22. Five days later, Danielle's badly decomposed body was found in a brushy rural area about 25 miles (40 km) from San Diego.

At the ensuing trial, lawyers hotly debated the question of when Danielle's body was deposited at the crime scene. Westerfield had been under constant police surveillance beginning February 4, and thus could not have murdered Danielle and/or moved the body after that time. Four forensic entomologists—David Faulkner, Haskell, Goff, and Hall—were called to give their separate determinations of time since colonization. Faulkner, who was part of the original CSI team, collected fourteen species of insects from on and around the body and testified for the defense. So did Hall and Haskell. Goff testified for the prosecution.

The bug experts were on the witness stand for four days and were subject to intense questioning by both prosecution and defense lawyers. All four experts reminded the jury that they could not say when Danielle died. They could only estimate the time the insects arrived at the body. All agreed that the infestation seemed lighter than might be expected for the locale and time of year. There were no studies to definitively explain that circumstance, but several possible explanations were presented. The fly population was low in 2002 because of a drought in Southern California. Warm, dry Santa Ana winds had blown for several days and could have quickly mummified Danielle's small body so that it was not attractive to flies. The body might have been covered for a time so insects could not get to it. A large ant population in the vicinity might have carried off many of the fly eggs prior to hatching.

Battle of the Experts

Because of the unknowns and two slightly different sets of temperature data taken from a nearby golf course and San Diego International Airport, the experts first disagreed on colonization times. Faulkner, Hall, and Haskell's dates all ruled out Westerfield's involvement, however. Faulkner found maggots whose size and stage of development led him to believe that Danielle's body had been colonized between February 16 and 18. "That's what the flies are telling me,"[90] he told the prosecutor during cross-examination.

Haskell was less precise in his estimate, and stated that the body had been colonized between February 14 and 21. Hall stated that he believed the flies had laid their eggs sometime between February 12 and February 23.

On the other hand, Goff believed that flies might have invaded Danielle's dead body as early as February 9. His credibility came under question when he was caught in a math error while on the stand, but he was able to explain convincingly

The CSI Effect

Forensic entomologist M. Lee Goff has served as an adviser for the TV series CSI: Crime Scene Investigation, *but many forensic experts have mixed feelings about such programs. Journalist Richard Willing explains why in his* USA Today *article, "'CSI Effect' Has Juries Wanting More Evidence":*

Prosecutors, defense lawyers and judges call it "the CSI effect," after the crime-scene shows that are among the hottest attractions on television. The shows . . . feature high-tech labs and glib and gorgeous techies. By shining a glamorous light on a gory profession, the programs also have helped to draw more students into forensic studies.

But the programs also foster what analysts say is the mistaken notion that criminal science is fast and infallible and always gets its man. . . . Real crime-scene investigators say that because of the programs, people often have unrealistic ideas of what criminal science can deliver. . . .

"You never see a case where the sample is degraded or the lab work is faulty or the test results don't solve the crime," says Dan Krane, president and DNA specialist at Forensic Bioinformatics in Fairborn, Ohio. "These things happen all the time in the real world."...

For all of *CSI*'s faults, some lab technicians say they have a soft spot for the TV version of their world. "It's great for getting people interested (in) careers' in forensic science," says Barbara Llewellyn, director of DNA analysis for the Illinois State Police.

Richard Willing, "'CSI Effect' Has Juries Wanting More Evidence," *USA Today,* August 5, 2004.

Forensic entomologist Dr. Neal Haskell on the witness stand during the David Westerfield murder trial in 2002.

that his analyses differed from the others because he used more recent data regarding maggot mass development. His estimation did not directly support the prosecution's theory that Danielle died as early as February 1, but it pushed the time of insect infestation closer to that early date.

The ambiguity and lack of consensus left lawyers frustrated, jurors confused, and some of the best forensic entomologists in the world looking foolish. Observers left the courthouse questioning the science itself, wondering if its value had been overrated. Goff defended it, however, saying: "The general public sometimes anticipates a little too much from us now, especially for court testimony. We can't always be a precise as they'd like if the evidence doesn't prove it."[91]

An Expanding Field

Courtroom battles may have caused the general public to question the value and trustworthiness of forensic entomology, but judges are convinced that the science is valid. They evaluate it using the Daubert standard, which stemmed from the 1993 benchmark Supreme Court case *Daubert v. Merrill Dow Pharmaceuticals*. Daubert established legal standards that an expert witness's testimony must meet before it can be accepted in court. Those standards state that the testimony has to be relevant and reliable to the case being tried, accepted by the expert's scientific peers, and based on disciplines which had been tested and written about in scientific journals. The insect experts' opinions measure up in every way.

While the courts value and accept insect evidence in the twenty-first century, the imprecision of that evidence illustrates that there is still much to be learned before forensic entomology can be termed an exact science. "It's not black and white. There's more play because of the environmental factors,"[92] reminds entomologist Richard Merritt.

The environmental factors and others will be better understood with the completion of more studies. Through them, variables that effect weather, temperature, and decomposition will be more thoroughly understood. Unidentified insects in every geographical region worldwide can be documented and studied. Researchers will also be able to address maggot mass metabolism, as well as issues ranging from the crossover of insects from carrion to a corpse to the effects of drug use on

Forensic entomologists are passionate about promoting the science of insects as well as the contributions that can be made to crime scene investigation.

insects at a variety of levels. Goff says, "The field is expanding into areas we had not thought possible only a few years ago. Our research is becoming more detailed, and advances in technology are necessitating a reexamination of many previous studies. Advances in computer technology and DNA research are opening areas not previously considered." [93]

Look to the Future

In just twenty years, forensic entomology developed from a little-known scientific subspecialty to a forensic tool that holds a great deal of promise. Those who work in the field are gratified that what was not even a profession in the 1970s now draws hundreds of young scholars who are excited about the practical side of the work. Goff says, "I have observed a phenomenal increase in the students majoring in forensic sciences. ... Significantly, these are students of very high caliber who may have earlier been looking at medicine or biology." [94]

Colleges and universities have begun offering forensic entomology classes and majors for those who are interested. From the University of Florida on the East Coast to Washington State University in the West, professors who are passionate about bugs are teaching crime scene techniques and taking their students on field trips to collect insects from decaying animal carcasses. Forensic entomologist Robert Kimsey at the University of California at Davis even introduces his students to the real thing—human corpses at the Sacramento County coroner's office. Kimsey remembers collecting maggots on the first field trip: "The stench was unbelievable. ... [But] you know what? [My students] did it. I was never so proud of any group of people in my life. Even the coroner's office people had a horrible time with this one. There were some serious reactions to it. But I was extremely proud of the way the students handled it. They did just a magnificent job." [95]

Forensic entomologists are passionate about promoting the science of insects as well as the contributions that can be made to crime scene investigation. Nevertheless, they never forget that they are—and will always be—only one small part of the criminal investigation team. They will uphold high standards, promote lofty goals, and try to speak clearly for the insects. After that, they must let others have the final say regarding guilt or innocence. Bass and science writer Jon Jefferson note, "[Investigators] and insects can reveal the truth about a crime, but they can't … guarantee that justice will be done. All they can do is serve as a voice for victims, and hope that voice is heard."[96]

Notes

Introduction: The Bug Detectives

1. Quoted in Anthony DeBartolo, "Fly Expert Lands Amid Murder," *Chicago Tribune*, July 12, 1988.

2. Quoted in DeBartolo, "Fly Expert Lands Amid Murder."

3. CSI: The Official DVD Collection Web site, "Web Interview M. Lee Goff, Entomology Expert." www.csicollection.com/interview04.php.

4. Quoted in Doug Moe, "Guess the Worst Science Job," *Capital Times* (Madison, Wisconsin), June 14, 2007.

5. Quoted in Jessica Snyder Sachs, "A Maggot for the Prosecution," *Discover*, November 1998, p. 102.

6. Quoted in Andrew Hermann, "It's the Flies That Bind Scientist, New Exhibit at Nature Museum:Former Professor Pioneered Using Bugs to Help Solve Crimes," *Chicago Sun-Times*, June 4, 2004.

7. Quoted in Rick Weiss, "Bug-Busters; the Insect Detectives," *Washington Post*, August 14, 1988.

8. Quoted in Martin Hall and Amoret Brandt, "Forensic Entomology," *Science in School*, Summer 2006, p. 53.

www.scienceinschool.org/repository/docs/issue2.pdf.

9. Quoted in William C. Hidlay, "Bugs and Flies Aren't Pests to This Forensic Expert," *Record* (New Jersey), September 6, 1987.

Chapter 1: Crime Scene Insects

10. M. Lee Goff, *A Fly for the Prosecution: How Insect Evidence Helps Solve Crimes*. Cambridge, MA: Harvard University Press, 2000, p. 25.

11. Duane Bourne, "Forensic Scientist Crawling with Knowledge of Insects," *Virginian-Pilot* (Norfolk, Virginia), November 17, 2005.

12. Emily Craig, *Teasing Secrets from the Dead*. New York: Crown, 2004, p. 50.

13. Quoted in BBC News, "Maggots Help Crack Perth Murder Mystery," BBC News, August 13, 2003. http://news.bbc.co.uk/1/hi/sci/tech/3144839.stm.

14. Quoted in Bill Godsil, "Crawling Clues; Bugs Can Help Determine Time When Person Died," *Richmond Times-Dispatch*, August 8, 2002.

15. SignOnSanDiego.com, "Transcript of David Westerfield Trial," SignOnSanDiego.com, July 10, 2002. /

www.signonsandiego.com/news/metro/danielle/transcripts/20020710-9999-pm1.html.

16. Quoted in Mark Gribben, "Enter the Cheese Skipper," truTV.com, 2008. www.crimelibrary.com/criminal_mind/forensics/kevin_neal/31.html.

17. Zakaria Erzinçlioğlu, *Maggots, Murder, and Men: Memories and Reflections of a Forensic Entomologist*. New York: Thomas Dunne, 2002, p. 90.

18. Quoted in Weiss, "Bug-Busters; the Insect Detectives."

19. Quoted in Sachs, "A Maggot for the Prosecution," p. 102.

20. Goff, *A Fly for the Prosecution*, p. 115.

21. Goff, *A Fly for the Prosecution*, p. 25.

22. Goff, *A Fly for the Prosecution*, p. 49.

23. Quoted in Why Files Web site, "CSI: Fly," Why Files Web site, July 14, 2005. http://whyfiles.org/014forensic/index.php?g=2.

24. Bill Bass and Jon Jefferson, *Death's Acre*. New York: Berkley, 2003, p. 99.

25. Jessica Snyder Sachs, *Corpse: Nature, Forensics, and the Struggle to Pinpoint Time of Death*. Cambridge, MA: Perseus, 2001, p. 112.

26. Quoted in John Mangels, "Scientist Studies Carcass to Help Catch Poachers," *Plain Dealer* (Cleveland, Ohio), June 24, 2007.

27. Goff, *A Fly for the Prosecution*, p. 54.

28. Goff, *A Fly for the Prosecution*, p. 55.

29. Quoted in Charles Slack, "Vial Meets Vile: Trail of Bugs Solves Puzzles of Death," *Richmond Times-Dispatch*, March 29, 1992.

30. Quoted in Bourne, "Forensic Scientist Crawling with Knowledge of Insects."

Chapter 2: A Gruesome Business

31. Quoted in Hidlay, "Bugs and Flies Aren't Pests to This Forensic Expert."

32. Quoted in J.B. Smith, "Baylor University Senior Jessie Toler Collects Insect Samples from a Dead Pig Wrapped in a Garbage Bag," *Waco Tribune-Herald* (Waco, Texas), May 21, 2004.

33. Goff, *A Fly for the Prosecution*, p. 152.

34. Quoted in Mangels, "Scientist Studies Carcass to Help Catch Poachers."

35. Goff, *A Fly for the Prosecution*, p. 43.

36. Quoted in Maria L. Chang, "Fly Witness: Forensic Entomologist Gail Anderson Helped Authorities Convict Two Poachers of Baby Black Bears by Studying Blowfly Eggs," *Science World*, October 1997. http://findarticles.com/p/articles/mi_m1590/is_n3_v54/ai_19986894/pg_1.

37. Bass and Jefferson, *Death's Acre*, p. 154.

38. Quoted in Weiss, "Bug-Busters; the Insect Detectives."

39. Quoted in John Sharp, "Insect Evidence: Forensic Entomology Uses Maggots to Determine Time and Place of Death in Homicide Cases," *Peoria Journal Star* (Peoria, Illinois), August 31, 2004.

40. Quoted in Mangels, "Scientist Studies Carcass to Help Catch Poachers."

41. Quoted in Sachs, *Corpse*, p. 80.

42. Goff, *A Fly for the Prosecution*, p. 161.

43. Claudia Dreifus, "The Fine Art of Watching a Bug's Life to Explain a Death," *New York Times*, January 2, 2007.

44. Quoted in Slack, "Vial Meets Vile."

45. Goff, *A Fly for the Prosecution*, p. 83.

46. Craig, *Teasing Secrets from the Dead*, p. 120.

47. Goff, *A Fly for the Prosecution*, p. 39.

48. Quoted in Martin E. Comas, "Bugs Help to Clarify Questions on Corpses: Scientists Study the Insects Eating Bodies to Determine the Time and Place of Death," *Orlando Sentinel*, July 12, 2005.

49. Quoted in Michael Baden and Marion Roach, *Dead Reckoning: The New Science of Catching Killers*. New York: Simon and Schuster, 2001, p. 155.

50. Quoted in SignOnSanDiego.com, "Transcript of David Westerfield Trial," SignOnSanDiego.com, July 30, 2002. www.signonsandiego.com/news/metro/danielle/transcripts/20020730-9999-pm1.html.

51. Goff, *A Fly for the Prosecution*, p. 63.

52. Goff, *A Fly for the Prosecution*, p. 63.

53. Quoted in Lawrence Osborne, "Crime-Scene Forensics: Dead Men Talking," *New York Times Magazine*, December 3, 2000, p. 105.

54. Quoted in Sachs, *Corpse*, p. 129.

55. Quoted in SignOnSanDiego.com, "Transcript of David Westerfield Trial," SignOnSanDiego.com, July 10, 2002. www.signonsandiego.com/news/metro/danielle/transcripts/20020710-9999-pm1.html.

56. Quoted in Harriet Ryan, "Bugs: The Best Witnesses?" Court TV News, July 18, 2002. www.courttv.com/trials/westerfield/071702_ctv.html.

Chapter 3: What the Bugs Reveal

57. Quoted in Bill Richards, "Bugs a Help in Pesky Murder Cases: Experts Gather Clues from (Yech!) Maggots, Other Insects Found in Bodies of Victims," *Rocky Mountain News* (Denver, Colorado), May 2, 1992.

58. Quoted in SignOnSanDiego.com, "Transcript of David Westerfield Trial," SignOnSanDiego.com, July 25, 2002. www.signonsandiego.com/news/metro/danielle/transcripts/20020725-9999-am2.html.

59. Quoted in Smith, "Baylor University Senior Jessie Toler Collects Insect Samples from a Dead Pig Wrapped in a Garbage Bag."

60. Goff, *A Fly for the Prosecution*, p. 62.

61. Quoted in Tom Nordlie, "Of Maggots and Murder: UF Researcher Says Sleuths Need New Way to Estimate Time of Death," *University of Florida*

News, July 26, 2007. http://news.ufl. edu/2007/07/26/maggot.

62. Goff, *A Fly for the Prosecution*, p. 60.

63. Stephen W. Bullington, "Case One," Forensic Entomology Web site, 1998. www.forensic-ent.com.

64. Quoted in Ralph Brave, "Let's Talk of Graves, of Worms," *UC Davis Magazine*, Summer 1999. http://ucdavismagazine.ucdavis. edu/issues/su99/Feature_Bugs2.html.

65. Quoted in Barbara Westlake-Kenny, "Examining the Evidence: DNA, Drugs, Hair—And Insects," *University of Alabama Magazine*, Fall 1999. http:// main.uab.edu/show.asp?durki=25348.

66. Quoted in BBC News, "Maggots Help Crack Perth Murder Mystery," BBC News, http://news.bbc.co.uk/1/hi/sci/ tech/3144839.stm.

67. Quoted in BBC News, "Maggots Help Crack Perth Murder Mystery."

68. Goff, *A Fly for the Prosecution*, p. 156.

69. Quoted in *Dallas Morning News*, "When Flies Aren't a Nuisance; They Aided Police in Attempted Murder Case, Expert Says," *Dallas Morning News*, December 14, 1990.

70. Goff, *A Fly for the Prosecution*, p. 186.

Chapter 4: What Affects the Bugs

71. Quoted in Jim Erickson, "The Crime Lab's Bug Man; Insects Help Solve Crimes, But, 'I'm the Only One Who Could Stomach This,'" *Arizona Daily Star*, August 10, 1991.

72. Goff, *A Fly for the Prosecution*, p. 7.

73. Goff, *A Fly for the Prosecution*, p. 32.

74. Quoted in *Science in School*, "Interview with a Forensic Entomologist," *Science in School*, Summer 2006, p. 52. www.scienceinschool. org/repository/docs/issue2.pdf.

75. Goff, *A Fly for the Prosecution*, p. 66.

76. Quoted in Jennifer V. Hughes, "Crawling with Clues: Exhibit Lays Out Bug Evidence That Has Helped to Solve Crimes," *Record* (Hackensack, New Jersey), June 23, 2006.

77. Goff, *A Fly for the Prosecution*, p. 13.

78. Goff, *A Fly for the Prosecution*, p. 145.

79. Quoted in Brian Albrecht, "'Bug Guy' Sees Beauty in Little Beasts," *Plain Dealer* (Cleveland, Ohio), February 24, 2006.

Chapter 5: Insects in Court

80. Goff, *A Fly for the Prosecution*, p. 177.

81. Quoted in Ryan, "Bugs: The Best Witnesses?"

82. Goff, *A Fly for the Prosecution*, p. 180.

83. Goff, *A Fly for the Prosecution*, p. 186.

84. Bass and Jefferson, *Death's Acre*, p. 250.

85. Quoted in Weiss, "Bug-Busters; the Insect Detectives."

86. Goff, *A Fly for the Prosecution*, p. 179.

87. Slack, "Vial Meets Vile."

88. Quoted in Mark Gribben, "After the Blow Flies Flew Away," truTV.com,

2008. www.crimelibrary.com/criminal_ mind/forensics/kevin_neal/30.html.

89. Quoted in Mark Gribben, "Counterpoint," truTV.com, 2008. www.crimelibrary.com/ criminal_mind/forensics/kevin_neal/36. html.

90. Quoted in Kristen Green, "Insect Evidence May Put Time of Death in Doubt," SignOnSanDiego.com, July 11, 2002. www.signonsandiego.com/ news/metro/danielle/20020711-9999_ 1n11davidw.html.

91. CSI: The Official DVD Collection Web site, "Web Interview M. Lee Goff, Entomology Expert."

92. Quoted in Harriet Ryan, "Bug for Bug: Prosecutors Hire Their Own Entomologist," Court TV News, July 15, 2002. www.courttv.com/trials/west-erfield/071502_ctv.html.

93. Nature Web Site, "Interview: Meet Forensic Entomologist M. Lee Goff," Nature Web Site, www.pbs.org/wnet/ nature/crimescene/interview.html.

94. Nature Web Site, "Interview: Meet Forensic Entomologist M. Lee Goff."

95. Quoted in Brave, "Let's Talk of Graves, of Worms."

96. Bass and Jefferson, *Death's Acre*, p. 110.

Glossary

accumulated degree hours (ADH): The product of time and temperature needed for insects to progress through developmental stages.

arthropods: Invertebrate animals of the phylum Arthropoda, including insects, crustaceans, arachnids (spiders), and myriapods (centipedes). All are characterized by a hard exoskeleton, a segmented body, and jointed limbs.

autopsy: Examination of a body to determine or confirm cause of death.

carrion: Dead animal flesh.

colonization: The establishment of a species in a new habitat, in this case a corpse.

differential decomposition: Accelerated decomposition, usually related to injuries.

ectotherm: An organism that regulates its body temperature largely by exchanging heat with its surroundings.

exoskeleton: A hard outer structure, such as the shell of an insect, that provides protection or support.

fauna: Animals (including insects) of a particular region.

faunal succession: The principle that insects are attracted to a corpse in a predictable order.

hemimetabolous: Undergoing incomplete metamorphosis.

holometabolous: Undergoing complete metamorphosis.

insects: 1. A major group of arthropods of the class Insecta, having an adult stage characterized by three pairs of legs; a body segmented into head, thorax, and abdomen; and usually two pairs of wings. Insects include flies, crickets, mosquitoes, beetles, butterflies, and bees. 2. Any of various similar arthropod animals, such as spiders, centipedes, or ticks.

instar: A stage of an insect or other arthropod between molts.

medicocriminal: Pertaining to medicine and crime.

molt: Periodic shedding of the cuticle.

necrophageous: Feeding on carrion or corpses.

parasitoid: Insects that spend a significant portion of their life within a single host, but on reaching maturity become free-living entities.

physiology: The biological study of the function of living organisms.

postmortem interval (PMI): The time between death and the discovery of a corpse.

pupa: Insect in the nonfeeding, usually immobile, transformation stage between the larva and adult, within a protective cocoon or hardened case.

species: The basic category of biological classification, composed of related individuals that resemble one another, are able to breed among themselves, but are not able to breed with members of another species.

spiracle: One of the outer openings of the respiratory system of certain invertebrates, usually on the sides of the body.

taxonomy: The science dealing with the description, identification, naming, and classification of organisms.

For More Information

Books

Danielle Denega, *Gut-Eating Bugs: Maggots Reveal the Time of Death!* Danbury, CT: Franklin Watts, 2007. An entertaining and easy-to-understand overview of forensic entomology.

Ron Fridell, *Forensic Science*. Minneapolis, MN: Lerner, 2007. An overview of modern-day crime scene investigation. Includes information on forensic entomology.

M. Lee Goff, *A Fly for the Prosecution: How Insect Evidence Helps Solve Crimes*. Cambridge, MA: Harvard University Press, 2000. A fascinating account of Goff's work as a forensic entomologist.

Sue Hamilton, *Forensic Entomology: Bugs & Bodies*. Edina, MN: ABDO, 2008. An informative look at forensic entomology.

Jessica Snyder Sachs, *Corpse: Nature, Forensics, and the Struggle to Pinpoint Time of Death*. Cambridge, MA: Perseus, 2001. Explores investigators' efforts to determine time of death using a variety of forensic evidence, including plants, bones, and insects.

Periodicals

Anthony DeBartolo, "Fly Expert Lands Amid Murder," *Chicago Tribune*, July 12, 1988.

Web Sites

American Board of Forensic Entomology (http://research.missouri.edu/entomology). Contains information about the American Board of Forensic Entomology, contact information and biographies for members, history of forensic entomology, case studies, and links to other entomology sites.

truTV (www.trutv.com). In-depth coverage of true crime cases, including that of Kevin Neal, in which forensic entomology played a large role.

Index

Picture Credits

About the Author

Diane Yancey lives in the Pacific Northwest with her husband, Michael; their dog, Gelato; and their cats, Newton, Lily, and Alice. She has written more than twenty-five books for middle-grade and high school readers, including *The Forensic Anthropologist*, *The Case of the Green River Killer*, *The Unabomber*, and *The Zodiac Killer*.